Spiritual
Development
for beginners

About the Authors

Professors Richard and Jan Potter are married and have taught at Dana College in Nebraska for over twenty years. Long-time students of the world's great spiritual traditions, they have studied intensively with accomplished meditation teachers and are experienced as spiritual guides. They have led workshops and seminars in the area of spiritual development.

Spiritual Development

for beginners

A Simple Guide to Leading a Purpose-Filled Life

RICHARD & JAN POTTER

Llewellyn Publications
Woodbury, Minnesota

FIRST EDITION
First Printing, 2006

Book design and layout by Joanna Willis
Cover design by Ellen Dahl
Cover flower image © Digital Stock
Cover background image © EyeWire
Illustration on page 53 by Llewellyn art department

Llewellyn is a registered trademark of Llewellyn Worldwide, Ltd.

Library of Congress Cataloging-in-Publication Data
Potter, Richard N., 1945–
    Spiritual development for beginners : a simple guide to leading a purpose-filled life / Richard & Jan Potter. — 1st ed.
        p. cm.
    Includes bibliographical references (p.   ) and index.
    ISBN-13: 978-0-7387-0750-1
    ISBN-10: 0-7387-0750-3
    1. Spiritual life. I. Potter, Jan, 1941– II. Title.

BL624.P6685 2006
204—dc22   2006047379

Llewellyn Worldwide does not participate in, endorse, or have any authority or responsibility concerning private business transactions between our authors and the public.
    All mail addressed to the author is forwarded but the publisher cannot, unless specifically instructed by the author, give out an address or phone number.
    Any Internet references contained in this work are current at publication time, but the publisher cannot guarantee that a specific location will continue to be maintained. Please refer to the publisher's website for links to authors' websites and other sources.

Llewellyn Publications
A Division of Llewellyn Worldwide, Ltd.
2143 Wooddale Drive, Dept. 0-7387-0750-3
Woodbury, MN 55125-2989, U.S.A.
www.llewellyn.com

Printed in the United States of America

Also by Richard Potter

Authentic Spirituality:
The Direct Path to Consciousness

For you, the reader, that your life
may be filled with love, harmony, and beauty.

Contents

Exercises

Introduction

You have just opened this book on spiritual development, and you may be wondering where it might lead you. For most of us, life is hectic and full of trials, along with moments of beauty and wonder. You may have picked up this book out of curiosity, but it is more likely that something is either calling you or pushing you. You may simply feel as if now is the time to take a new leap forward, or you may be in the middle of a huge crisis that has pushed you close to the end of your endurance. Perhaps your usual ways of dealing with life are no longer working as well as they used to work. Old formulas for understanding your life's meaning and figuring out your purpose may seem dry and not very fruitful. Many of us start to think more seriously about spiritual development when we are in such places.

Even though you may feel a tremendous need to try something new, you may have little time for endeavors that sound time-consuming or daunting. Perhaps spiritual development falls in the latter category for you, yet something beckons you to move on. Like the tiny ruby-throated hummingbird that is at this moment hovering above the feeder outside our window as night falls, we are drawn to that which is nourishing for us. Just a few sips of the nectar from the hummingbird feeder will carry this tiny, jewel-like bird through the long night until he can awaken and whirl into motion in the morning. We are surprised that he is here so late, as it's already a bit hard to see in the twilight. Yet his need for nourishment propels him, and here he is, now darting about, now sipping, now resting for a moment on the top of the feeder.

What is it that draws you? What nourishes your body, your mind, your heart, and your soul? Like the hummingbird, you may feel as though you fly here and there, hoping for real nourishment, yet that nourishment seldom appears. Authentic sources of nectar for our spiritual lives are hard to find, and we often are disappointed. Still, this universe is a place of deep compassion for all seekers, and underneath the surface of life runs a deep, clear river of hope, joy, peace, and healing that is available to all who venture there. Our purpose in writing this book is to provide you with tools for deep self-discovery, as well as maps for some of the many paths to the life-giving river. We will look at some of the ways in which the world of spiritual meaning may open up to us. We will explore the unknown treasure of latent spiritual resources that all of us carry within, and we will suggest ways to access that treasure. Despite all the heartbreak and absurdities of life in the twenty-first century, there is still an all-pervading compassion that is waiting for each of us to find the courage to begin this great adventure. Whenever you decide to make the journey—or whenever you wish to deepen the work you have already begun—you will find that help is available to you, despite the apparent obstacles.

This book is the result of many journeys, and yet it offers fresh, new, uniquely personal avenues for your exploration. As Richard's previous book, *Authentic Spirituality: The Direct Path to Consciousness,* suggests, many of the traditional paths for spiritual development appear to be insufficient for the needs of contemporary people, yet we still may learn from the journeys of the many who have gone before us. The journey is ancient, yet it is ever-changing, and we cannot assume anything. Your experience will be different from anyone else's, which is what will make this such a great adventure.

Our knowledge is grounded in the collective experience and wisdom of the thousands who have courageously followed a myriad of paths to find the spiritual nectar they have longed for—sometimes desperately, sometimes lovingly, sometimes hopefully, and sometimes just because they could see no other option. These adventurers were usually ahead of their times, and they were often regarded as marginal—sometimes even outcasts—in their societies. We may learn from their experiences, as some of what we go through today follows patterns similar to those of others, even though the details may be different.

Some spiritual paths are ancient and well traveled, and some spiritual adventures are new and fresh, revealing themselves from moment to moment. Each person's journey is unique; at every step you take, you will be creating your own path. What we offer you in this book is a couple of friends to walk beside you as you begin your journey of spiritual development, a journey that will unfold for you according to your own unique needs, your gifts, the deepest desires of your heart, and the purpose of your life. Wherever you are in your journey, you have within you rich possibilities beyond your imagination. We will share with you what we have learned from our own journeys and what we have learned from the journeys of others, always honoring your own inner wisdom, your own ability to discern what is right for you. We live in an era in which we can no longer depend on great teachers to show us the way. In this time, we are guided by our own inner radar, much as the tiny hummingbird finds its way from our yard to Central America each winter. There are authentic teachers here and there, but the ultimate guide for the journey lies within each of us.

One of the stories we like best relates spiritual development to the search for life-giving water. We can find water virtually anywhere on this planet—*if* we are willing to dig deep enough. There are some places where the water is closer to the surface and we do not have to dig quite so far to quench our thirst as we might elsewhere. The quality of the water varies from place to place as well. Sometimes the water we find tastes sweet and pleasant, and sometimes it is bitter and hard to swallow. How might you know where to dig? And how might you find tools that are effective and efficient to use in your inner work? In this book, we intend to assist you in discovering the best places to start digging for the water that will sustain you on your journey of spiritual growth, and we also will give you some ideas about the tools that might serve you well as you dig.

Spiritual development is a many-faceted endeavor, and you may be surprised by the multitude of paths and practices that can lead you to wonderful discoveries. The table of contents of this book will give you an idea of the different doors that we plan to open for you. An example of one of the useful ways we have found to speed your growth is to focus on qualities that, when developed in your personality, will help you to attain your goals in life. You may have heartfelt dreams that you figure you could never make real, because you think that you do not have what it takes to succeed in these areas. Yet the reality is that all of us carry within us the seeds of latent qualities that we can bring to life to enrich our personalities and to achieve our purposes. Various spiritual practices and exercises will help you to identify these qualities, strengthen them, and integrate them into your personality. As you develop qualities that you did not know you possessed, you will find yourself gradually transformed into a person who can accomplish goals that once seemed unattainable. Look at the ends of sections or chapters of this book for exercises that will assist you in this work.

The realization of your spiritual potential in life involves cultivating the head and the heart as well as many other facets of your being. It calls for accessing new knowledge, learning new skills, and taking leaps of faith into realms that you may not have yet explored. To unfold the richness of your being, you may find yourself holding a mirror to your own self to learn who you really are, and you may dare to look at the shadow that each of us possesses in order to mine the treasures hidden there. You may choose the paths that feel best for you. The many possibilities include learning to meditate, working with dreams, developing your own spiritual practices, going deep into the world of relationships, and connecting more profoundly with Nature. You will learn how to polish your heart and bring it to life so that your entire being will feel more alive and radiant. We wish you a pleasant journey and many fine discoveries!

one

What Is Spirituality?

Each person has a different constellation of reasons for being attracted by the notion of spiritual development. Perhaps it may be time for you to take another step in the unfolding of your being, or maybe you have hit a dead end in your life and know it is time for something different. Possibly you have been through a difficult period, with tremendous challenges or painful personal losses, or perhaps you are simply frustrated with what appears to be the lack of authentic, commonsense approaches to finding deeper purpose and meaning in your life. All of these are among the many reasons for thinking about your spiritual development. Before we proceed, however, we need to look at what we mean by "spirituality."

Spirituality may be seen as the purposeful changing of consciousness to provide more access to varying mental perspectives, subtler levels of experience, deeper awareness of self, the opening and awakening of the heart, a wider array of emotional experiences, and states of consciousness that connect with subtle realms of being. Spirituality shatters our set convictions about the nature of life on the rock of Truth. Spirituality is all about experience. It expands the range of acceptable experience by opening consciousness to more of life. Indeed, most of us walk around in a bubble of highly constricted experience, cut off from the vast, amazing, and beautiful life around us. Spirituality awakens us to life—usually gradually, but occasionally quickly.

Spirituality is also about the interpretation of what we experience. Some interpretations of experience lead to constricting our worlds, and some lead to further expansion and exploration of life. Interpretation of experience comes in many forms. Some of these forms are religious, some are scientific, some are mystical, and many lie in the myriad of spaces among these perspectives. Opportunity for authentic spirituality may be found in all of these interpretations, as long as they serve as doorways into further exploration and are not literalized door-closers attempting to stamp out continued searching for deeper experience and meaning.

Spirituality, Meaning, and Purpose in Life

You may wonder if there is a connection between spirituality and your sense of purpose and meaning in life. The answer is a resounding "Yes!"

For most of us, finding meaning in our lives and having a sense of purpose are critical to our everyday experience of well-being. Getting up in the morning can be a huge struggle if you cannot identify a purpose that calls you. On the other hand, if your life makes sense to you and if you find meaning in what you do every day, then you probably can make it through the most terrible catastrophes that life brings to you.

We have found that we can weather virtually any storm if our sense of meaning and purpose is intact. The in-between places in life, the transitional periods that all of us go through—these are the times when we often question what it is all about. You may ask, "Why am I here on this planet?" You may want to know why there is so much suffering in the world. Old explanations may make no sense to you anymore. You many wonder, "What is the use of trying so hard, when everything I do seems to turn out so rotten?" Sometimes the world turns empty and gray when a few days or weeks ago it was bright and joyful. The difference between the two states may relate to a loss of meaning, a loss of the sense of the purposefulness of life. A deep spiritual life can help you to hang on to meaning and purpose, although it is true that these change as you grow, and the transitions will sometimes still be tough. We will talk more about this later in the book.

Spirituality may help you to find a deeper meaning in your life, as well as a clearer sense of purpose, in many ways. One of them relates to learning methods for transcending your daily struggles so that you may gain more perspective on what is happening in your life. A wonderful gift to yourself is to go on a spiritual retreat for a few days, a week, or even a month. Getting away from daily routines so that you can raise your consciousness enough to see your life in a different context almost always transforms the way you understand the meaning of your life, and it usually helps you to see how your purpose is unfolding.

Simply meditating for thirty minutes or so every morning may lift your spirits and your consciousness, create a tranquil space, and help you to see that there is indeed meaning in your daily experiences. You may find that these experiences are fulfilling a larger purpose that you may not see in the midst of ordinary tasks and struggles. When Jan's two sons were little, she told them that she needed to meditate each morning in order to be more happy and calm. She would go into a little room to meditate but always left the door slightly open, and usually one of the boys would come in for a while, sit on her lap while she was meditating, and then leave whenever he was ready. If one of them needed something or had a question, she dealt with it, but they respected that space. It was a sweet experience that she still remembers fondly. When the boys reached the ages of perhaps five and seven years old, they would sometimes remind Jan how important meditation was. If something went wrong and she started to get flustered, one of them might say, "Mommy, maybe you need to go meditate." They got it!

Accessing the world of spirituality may help you to create peaceful spaces within, where you may find a richness of being that you have not encountered before. Rather than making you "spacey," this spiritual world has the potential to help you free your spirit from the incessant demands of the world while grounding you in the firm foundation of your everyday life. From this place, you may find a clearer and more joyful sense of your purpose in life, and you may encounter supportive new companions who share your perspective. The next chapter, "Spiritual Development," will describe more fully how this process unfolds.

two

Spiritual Development

Even though each of us must create our own unique spiritual path, there are well-developed techniques for developing consciousness that have formed the corpus of spiritual paths for thousands of years. Because of cultural factors, these methods may look different in various parts of the world. The inner, transformative aspects are the same, because they apply to the universal human condition. Once you get past surface things, we are all human beings and share a common inner geography. We are also uniquely individual, and each of us will follow a path that is different from that of any other person. A spiritual path, then, is a blend of common features with room for individual difference. It is equally true that we *find* our paths and that we *create* our paths. Several years ago, Richard wrote the following story, which gives some insight into our path. Amidst the symbols of the story, you may find both common human characteristics and aspects unique to our specific journey of discovery.

Waking Up

Once upon a time, I woke up—I wasn't completely awake, just awake enough to know that I had been asleep. It wasn't exactly clear-headed-and-ready-to-go wakefulness, but more like groggy-and-barely-there wakefulness. I found myself in a huge room. I looked around and saw that I was in the midst of thousands, maybe millions, of people, mostly asleep, yet busy with their somnambulistic lives. Everyone was making some sort of noise and was occupied with various activities that made no sense to me. I wondered how long I had been asleep. Maybe I had been awake sometime before, or maybe not—I couldn't quite remember. The realization that just a few minutes ago I had most likely been sleepwalking like those around me, making useless noises and engaged in odd behavior, made me shiver and want to run. Instead, I began to observe this strange scene.

Everyone around me was running hither and yon, engaged in activities that appeared meaningless but seemed to them to be matters of great import. All of them were making strange sounds—everyone had a noise or sound that was unique. Many of the sounds seemed to clash with the others around them, and when that happened, the people only seemed to make their noises louder and their activities more frenetic, apparently trying to drown out the sounds being made by others. I was reminded of a dream I thought I might have had (or was that during another period of wakefulness?) about a beautiful choir at the center of a gigantic room, where all of the voices combined in harmony and all activities blended into a peaceful, brilliant light.

I began to wander into the crowd. While many people were doing their own thing around the periphery, I noticed that there were others who had focused on a particularly loud and magnetic individual and were trying to emulate that person. The sounds they made were not soothing but drew me toward them because of the volume. Just before I was caught by the group's magnetism, I broke away because of a vague memory of having tried this many times before in my sleepwalking state; it was completely unsatisfying. As I continued my walk, I saw many more groups of loud and discordant people.

I sat for a while and watched a particularly interesting scenario unfold. As I sat there, a beautiful and magnetic individual emerged from the center of the room. His activities were less frantic than others, and his sound was clear, well developed, and beautiful. He stood among the crowds, and since he spoke a language that no one else understood, he pointed toward the center and sang his beautiful note. Then he left. The people who had been drawn to him were startled. They wanted him to return and take them with him. They cried and carried on until finally one of them drew a picture of his pointing finger and hung it where he had been standing. The crowd that had gathered began to worship the picture. They said that he would return one day and take them with him to some other world. No one thought to look in the direction in which he had been pointing. Soon they were carrying the picture around to other groups and trying to get others to worship the pointing finger. By this time, the picture could be pointing in any direction; no one noticed or cared. I suddenly saw from afar the object of all of this veneration, now unnoticed and standing quietly near the peaceful center of the vast room. He was watching all of this and looked profoundly sad. He noticed that I was watching him, and he smiled at me. His smile was so deep that it wrenched my heart from my chest and bathed it in the waters of his tears. I felt profound sadness, but I also discovered the strength to move away from the periphery of the room and toward the center.

When I moved toward the center, things became quieter, and people were less frenetic. People here were working harder on harmonizing their voices, and occasionally there were glimpses of beauty in their sounds and movements. Here, too, there were people who formed into groups centered around magnetic individuals, but the sounds that emanated from them were gentler, and their activities less agitated. I stopped for a while and enjoyed the harmonious sounds and gentle people in one of these groups. It seemed like a

way station where I could drop some of the inner barriers that I had developed to protect myself from the
gross noises and unfriendly people around the periphery of the room.

That is where I met her. She had been waiting for
me. From the moment we met, we knew that our
destiny was to complete the journey to the center
together. Our songs were inseparable and in harmony. We stayed with this group for a while in order to heal and learn. One day, while sitting at the
quiet outskirts of the group, we heard the faint echo
of an exquisite sound coming from the center of the
vast room. Our hearts leaped, the sadness of ages
left, and we felt powerful hope and joy. We suddenly
were filled with the desire to find the sound and light
at the center. Feeling like moths drawn to a flame,
we wanted to become one with the sounds there. Together, we left the group of kind souls and walked
toward the center.

Soon the faint echo we had heard turned into a
great crescendo of music that filled our minds and
hearts. Then we were standing before an incredible, vast white light, bright beyond description, that
seemed to be connected to the deep and profound
sound. We remembered warnings that one could not
enter the center and live. People had said that, like
moths in a flame, we would be extinguished. They
had said that we should not go near this place but
rather let authorities describe their opinions about

it to us. Instead, we looked at each other, smiled, and stepped into the vast light. This was our purpose: to wake up together or to die trying.

Everything was just as it had been, yet it was completely different. At first, it seemed that everything that we had known was gone and that we were adrift in a new world. Then we got our bearings and began to get used to this new world, somehow existing within the old, familiar world. We realized that wakefulness is not extinction, nor is it emergence into a completely different world. Instead, we simply started to live our song in the midst of sleepwalkers, those who are partially awake, and a few we discovered who had also made the journey.

You've probably picked up this book because you are interested in furthering your spiritual development. Possibly, you picked it up out of curiosity. For whatever reason, you are about to embark upon a quest that will, without a doubt, change you. If you read this book and do the exercises included, you will experience changes that go beyond simply having more information. You will be at risk of changing your perspective, priorities, feelings, and behaviors—and your consciousness. These changes are what spiritual development is all about. The changes that occur are real, although they usually happen gradually. They are noticeable, even in the early stages, and will make a significant difference in the quality of your life.

Changing Priorities

As you purposefully choose to develop spiritually, you may find that your priorities shift, at least on a conscious level. Materialistic priorities, though not necessarily dropping completely away, will begin to recede in favor of priorities related to spiritual progress. Priorities related to dulling consciousness, like spending hours in shopping malls or partying every weekend, may be replaced by the desire to sharpen your perceptions, such as spending time in Nature or your garden. Richard remembers a telling example from his own experience:

> I had just been initiated into the Sufi Order of the West by Pir Vilayat Inayat Khan after a Wednesday-evening lecture in Chicago. On the next Friday evening, before I was going to participate in a weekend workshop with him in Madison, Wisconsin, I played poker and drank beer with friends. On Saturday, I had an interview with Pir Vilayat to receive spiritual practices. The first thing he said to me was, "Where were you last night?" His quiet but powerful words penetrated my heart, and for the next five years I abstained from alcohol. This does not mean that you cannot drink anything besides water in order to be on a spiritual path. Rather, I chose not to drink alcoholic beverages until I knew who was in charge of all of my activities.

Typically, the most difficult part of changing priorities is that it makes the people around you nervous, sometimes upset. Friends are usually formed around shared interests and activities. When you change those interests and activities, your friends may begin to feel left out, or even rejected. If you are married or in a relationship, your partner may begin to feel that he or she is no longer as important to you as before and may need reassurance that you still care.

Sometimes it may be necessary to loosen ties with friends who seek to drag you back into your old priorities, but, if possible, it is preferable to transform these relationships through love, patience, and example. When we speak to groups of people who are seeking to transform their consciousness and grow spiritually, many of the questions asked revolve around the loss that people feel as they find themselves drifting away from old friends and as they discover their desire to connect with new friends who will share their priorities. Change, especially spiritual change, naturally involves sacrifice from time to time. It is not necessary to seek sacrifice; it will come occasionally as the natural result of the changes in what you do, think, and choose as you pursue your spiritual path.

Change in Perspective

Spiritual development is dependent upon changing your perspective. There are three primary directions that your consciousness may take when changing perspective. These directions, which we will discuss below, are *high*, *broad*, and *deep*.

Going high has often been the primary direction people think about when considering a change in perspective that might be more spiritual. Using images like mountain peaks and the stars, we seek a perspective that takes us above our daily lives and troubles. We seek to get above those things so that we may see the overall picture of our lives, or maybe the interwoven causes behind events, or possibly the greater purposes of our lives. The perspective of height helps us to detach from the pull of life, and especially from emotions, so that we can temporarily understand the demands of life without being overwhelmed by our location in the midst of life. It is useful to get high through the use of spiritual practices in order to set priorities and to avoid being overwhelmed by the pressing demands of life. Going high may become a cop-out—often called a spiritual bypass—if we use it to avoid dealing with the inevitable messiness of everyday life. For this reason, going high needs to be only one of the ways in which you work to change your perspective.

Broadening your perspective through empathy and creative imagination is another way to change consciousness. It happens when you take the time to listen to those around you and try to understand their perspectives as if they were your own. It happens when you watch all the beings around you and attempt to see the world through their experiences. It happens when not only people but also animals, plants, and even minerals speak to you. With these experiences, you are making your horizon wider and wider. You are opening your heart to life, and life will reward you with increased harmony, vision, and wisdom.

Deepening your perspective will take you into the occasionally treacherous realms of your deeper emotions and those aspects of your being of which you are not aware. Most of us live cut off from much of our capacity for feeling and are quite unaware of the totality that comprises our true selves. When you deepen your perspective, you discover sublime treasures as well as some issues that you have feared deep within, hidden from your conscious awareness. Life becomes rich, and you become more powerful when emotion and hidden qualities are discovered and integrated into your awareness.

Some religious groups project the more negative aspects of the deep onto nonbelievers or "evil creatures" and claim only virtues for their adherents; unfortunately, this leads to two major problems. The first is that this perspective cripples spiritual development by making wholeness impossible, and the second is that the tradition is eventually dominated or threatened by the very traits that it rejects, as those shadow qualities refuse to stay hidden forever. When exploring various spiritual paths, you should always be wary of unbalanced ones that do not provide the means to explore all three of these perspectives.

Spiritual Practices

In addition to changing your priorities and perspectives, doing spiritual practices will become integral to your spiritual development. A spiritual practice is one of a vast repertoire of carefully designed activities that seekers use for the purpose of spiritual growth. They are the means by which you change your priorities and perspectives, but they may also help you to reach a multitude of other goals, such as developing your ability to concentrate, strengthening your mind, enhancing your intuition, awakening your heart, and refining aspects of your personality. Spiritual practices work in a variety of ways, but in general, they quicken dormant qualities in your being so that these qualities may manifest in your personality and in your life.

Virtually all traditions have spiritual practices of some sort that are used for spiritual development. In some cases, they are used only to create states of reverence, joy, exaltation, or peace in order to draw the seeker into a deeper relationship with the representatives (both corporeal and noncorporeal) of that tradition. In schools of spiritual study, spiritual practices are used to train the mind and emotions to do the work of building the spiritual self. Here, too, spiritual states of joy, exaltation, ecstasy, love, and peace are invoked—but for the purpose of achieving deep understanding and spiritual liberation.

You will be introduced to many spiritual practices in the chapters to follow. You will find it useful to view them as tools for accomplishing the purposes for which they are prescribed—not as ends in themselves. Practices are a gift and may be compared with the concept of grace. If you do the practices diligently, they will work. Spiritual practices are quite magical in that they work invisibly on levels you are seldom aware of, and yet in time they will transform you. At first, you may hardly notice the changes brought about by spiritual practices, because these changes are incremental, and yet whatever changes you seek almost always will occur. They may not happen exactly as you expect, however, because spiritual practices invoke energies that are wiser than we are. Be careful what you ask for, though, because you are liable to get it—intentions are powerful.

If you approach spiritual practices with humility, with the intention of making yourself an accommodation for the beauty of the universe and for the deeper qualities of inner realms, most likely you will be rewarded with great gifts. There is a paradox involved here: you must work at the practices to accomplish anything, yet at a certain point all you can do is relax, surrender to the practices, and allow them to work on you. The more you are able to get your limited self—the part of you that some call the ego—out of the way, the more quickly the practices will work. Emptying yourself of expectations and pride prepares the way for the fulfillment of spiritual awakening.

Who Will Benefit from Spiritual Development?

You may be wondering whether you are the sort of person who can benefit from doing spiritual practices. Many people from a wide variety of perspectives may gain much from studying spiritual development. Whether you are a "born contemplative" and are looking for an opening into mystical studies, an agnostic who finds it difficult to relate to most religions, or a member of a mainstream religious organization, you will find the approach and the knowledge contained in these pages useful. Let's briefly explore each of these three starting points for a seeker.

It may be that after leaving your childhood, you have found it difficult to relate to the claims of exclusivity and the culturally encapsulated nature of the religion into which you were born. Religious doctrine may leave you feeling empty, since you are looking for something that is alive and transforming. You may also feel uncomfortable with a solely materialistic alternative to religion. Maybe you have had psychic experiences that others around you laughed at or found weird. Possibly you found that what moved and motivated others left you wondering, "What's all the fuss?" What moves you and makes life meaningful for you may be more internal, or may be related to Nature, or may involve stories and myths. If you resonate with some of the above descriptions, you may have a leaning toward the mystical. In this case, you will find this book useful as an introduction to spiritual development—or possibly as a refresher course.

If you have never found religion to be something to which you could relate, possibly because it seemed too simplistic or unrealistic, yet you hold out some hope that there is meaning beyond science and the visible, you may call yourself an agnostic or even an atheist. Both of these deny the sort of God that, like Santa Claus, is watching your every move—or even the deistic, remote God that became popular a couple of centuries ago. Agnosticism states that there is no God that one can believe in, because any true God is unknowable; atheism denies the existence of a God. But neither position negates the possibility of transcendent reality. In spite of the overliteralized, chauvinistic, fear-promoting components of many religions, spirituality lives on, and individuals may touch the ineffable Oneness of being without believing in a God of any sort. You need not believe in a particular doctrine to engage in spiritual development; just experiment with the knowledge and practices contained in this book and see what changes occur in your life.

You may be a person who feels deeply attuned to your particular faith tradition, and yet you may find yourself yearning for ways to deepen your spiritual attunement and may wish to take positive steps toward spiritual development. You might discover that the knowledge and practices contained in this book are not foreign to your tradition, but rather they are part of the tradition that has been either lost or suppressed over the ages. Spiritual development has been a part of all traditions, yet at times the knowledge has been lost because of persecution, war, or intrigue. Sometimes religious officials have sought to keep deep spiritual knowledge private in order to keep the populace dependent upon them. Now, however, much information is readily available to those who choose to look for it. It may be that mainstream religions would do well to incorporate spiritual development as part of their teachings in order to offer a more profound experience to members and to provide an alternative to the fundamentalist sects that are draining many mainstream congregations of those desiring a powerful spiritual experience. If you are seeking to expand and deepen your spiritual life while remaining a faithful participant in your church, synagogue, mosque, or temple, you may do so through the application of the information in this book.

Heart's Desire Exercise:
What Do You Really Want?

At this point, you may ask yourself, "Why? What might be the benefits of spiritual development? Does spiritual development fit with my deepest heart's desire?" Here is a list of some of the benefits. Your task is to contemplate the benefits and decide whether this is what you deeply want. There is a cost for everything we do. If you work on spiritual development, you may sacrifice aspects of some other arena of life, because your priorities will change. Will the rewards be likely to compensate for the changes? In other words, what is it that you truly desire?

Here is a brief list for contemplation of some of the possible outcomes of committing yourself to spiritual development:

- *Wisdom*—Wisdom is like the horizon; there is always further to go. You will grow in wisdom the longer you pursue self-knowledge and develop consciousness. Wisdom is not only of the mind but also belongs to the living heart.

- *Joy*—Joy is the natural state for awakened individuals. You may be more awake to the suffering of the world, but joy will become your default mode. Joy that bubbles up from the heart, regardless of external conditions, is characteristic of so many spiritually advanced individuals.

- *Peace*—Peace is the twin of joy, although there is often some tension between the two. Under the fullness of

a joyful heart lies an ocean of quiet peace that transcends all duality.

- *Magnetism*—As you grow spiritually, it shows, and
  people are often drawn to you. (This may be subtle,
  and at some point you may need to veil your magnetism out of humility and the wish to allow others to
  determine their own lives.)

- *Healing*—As you awaken, your presence gradually
  becomes more healing to everything and everyone
  around you.

- *Connectedness*—You will experience a deeper relationship with the inner nature of the world around
  you. People, places, animals, plants, stones—all
  things will begin to speak to you as you become
  more aware of your connections.

What you truly want may be a bit clearer to you now.
You may wish to continue to think about identifying your
deepest heart's desire. As you make decisions about your
goals for the future, it is wise to listen to the voice of your
heart, balanced with the clarity of your mind. In the next
chapter, we will describe a number of different paths for
spiritual development.

three

Is There a Map?

As you think about the notion of spiritual development, you may ask the question, "Is there a map for this journey, or am I on my own?" You may wonder, "Is there a pattern of development that everyone experiences?" There are a myriad of answers to these questions. Everyone sees these issues through different lenses, and most are probably right. Our answer is, "It all depends." It depends on your own conscious intention, it depends on your heart's desire, and it depends on your level of commitment. In our experience, each person's path of spiritual development is unique, yet there are some patterns that tend to hold true.

A number of researchers from different spiritual backgrounds have studied these questions, and they have come up with some similar answers. Jan has interviewed people from various spiritual backgrounds who have been committed to their spiritual paths for at least fifteen or twenty years, and she found some patterns that were similar to those of the previous researchers and some experiences that did not fit previous descriptions. On the basis of this research, as well as our observations and our own experiences over the past thirty years, we believe that there are some truths about spiritual development that we can pass on to you. Yet ultimately, each person's journey is unlike any other. We will explore some of the patterns, but you must remember that none of them may be exactly like your own experience.

One of the reasons for the tremendous variety in the ways people grow spiritually is that spirituality itself is such an ineffable thing. Some speak of the process in terms of "growing your soul" (or "making a soul"), a lovely phrase but one that is difficult to describe, as the concept of soul is used in so many different ways. You may be challenged to grow in virtually any arena of your life, often where you least expect to encounter spiritual lessons or powerful experiences. All of life is permeated by spirit, so all of life is a potential teacher. Most of us constantly receive spiritual guidance from life, yet we may miss that guidance, because we just do not expect it to be there. Spiritual guidance and opportunities for growth may emerge from your experiences with family, friends, love relationships, work, Nature, financial dealings, education, travel, organizations, spiritual and religious groups, and even health challenges. An aspect of your life may suddenly become numinous, permeated with meaning, and you may find yourself expanding in directions that are totally surprising to you. Whatever happens to you, whoever comes into your life—all of this, pleasant or difficult, may contain an opening for learning and growth. The point is to be aware, to expect that at any time something meaningful could happen.

Peeling the Onion

One metaphor for spiritual development is that of gradually letting go of baggage, stripping layers off that which we call "the self." According to this thinking, little by little, we let unnecessary layers of ourselves fall away, a bit like peeling an onion. The goal is to get down to the "essential self," that part of our being that is true and real. The parts that fall away are seen as coverings that we take on as we respond to the socialization that all of us experience as we grow up. We learned as children to think and behave in ways that were usually acceptable to our parents, our school teachers, our religious leaders, and various other community persons and groups whose opinions mattered to us. The interesting thing is that we often mistake these coverings for our true selves; we forget that they are external to our deeper selves. While these coverings may serve us well during certain periods of our lives, at the point when we yearn to become more authentic, they may hold us back. Then the time has come to peel them off, or to let them fall away. Timing is everything, as moving too fast can be frightening and even counterproductive.

You may find that you can jump-start the process by choosing to let go of something that is no longer necessary to your life. An example that might be relevant for some would be letting go of the tendency to talk about other people when you hang out with friends. You might decide that you do not feel particularly good about this practice and then try to stop doing it for a week or a month. There's a pretty good chance that once you have made this effort, you will not want to go back to talking about people when they are not present. A consequence may be that you feel more authentic as a human being. When you see folks that you might have wanted to talk about, you can look them in the eye and feel good, as you have nothing to hide and nothing to feel guilty about. A bonus is that this increases your personal magnetism. A layer of the onion has fallen away! (Chapter 10, "Developing Mastery," discusses this theme further.)

In another scenario, after you have committed yourself to the adventure of spiritual development, you will find that there are things that don't matter as much to you as they used to. You might now feel that if you do not get chosen to head a team or take a certain kind of leadership role at work or in an organization to which you belong, you will be seen as "less than." Consequently, you strive to be recognized as bright and capable by speaking up at meetings, confronting others, or working exceedingly hard. One day, you may suddenly realize that this does not matter as much to you anymore. You know who you are, and whether or not the people around you constantly reinforce your self-worth by putting you in responsible positions or telling you how capable you are is beside the point. You relax a bit, and you begin to feel more centered and grounded. A layer of the onion has just fallen away—and you did not have to do much to make it happen. Your intention has initiated the process.

Making the Journey

The metaphor of "the journey" has been used for thousands of years by spiritual seekers, and for good reason. Seekers of many different persuasions have found that their spiritual experiences felt like a great adventure, a great journey whose goal kept shifting the farther they traveled. Some may have started their journeys because their lives were wrecks, they felt desperate, and they had to do something—anything—to escape the despair. Others may have leaped onto their paths because someone inspired them by deep words of wisdom, by a powerful presence, by glorious music, or by a kind gesture. Their thoughts may have been, "If only I could be like this person!" Still others may have come to the end of a phase of their lives—one of those hazy transition points—with the realization, "There must be more to life than this," and the search began.

You may find yourself in one of these places; maybe you have traveled down one of these roads. Whatever your initial goal might have been, it usually will change as the journey progresses. When you hike down a trail, the horizon shifts, and so it is with a spiritual journey. As you deepen and get more in touch with your heart's desire, what you aspired to at the beginning of the path changes. What you really want turns out to be different from what you once thought you wanted, and so your journey takes new turns, with delightful surprises, unforeseen trials, and beautiful realizations.

While we realize that many of the traditions of the past may have outlived their usefulness, there are some parts of those traditions that may be helpful to some of us. The spiritual growth maps of various mystical traditions are examples. Buddhists, Christians, Sufis, Hindus, indigenous shamanic traditions, and others have developed highly sophisticated maps for spiritual journeys, and while they do not fit everyone, they may be lifesavers at certain points. The Zen ox pictures (Reps 1989) are a wonderful example. The pictures are a series of drawings that illustrate the most common stages of a spiritual journey, according to the Zen tradition. Even though this is an old tradition, the drawings carry a fresh energy that still communicates to us today. When we use them in talks to groups, we find that most people easily relate to them.

The Sufi initiatory path, while varying from school to school, provides guides, generally in the oral tradition, that lay out stages of spiritual development that seem to transcend time. Most people whom we have guided or observed generally go through some variation on these stages. Western researchers who have tried to study people's spiritual growth patterns have come up with stages that have some commonalities with the Zen and Sufi stages, as well as with other spiritual stage models. The main difference is that the models developed by Western exoteric researchers tend to stop at what other models see as intermediate stages.

One of the most useful aspects of referring to spiritual development models or maps is that they help you to discern whether what you are experiencing is part of a common stage of spiritual development, whether it may signify that you are in a transition place between stages, or whether your experience is "off the map" of what others have experienced in their spiritual growth.

The transition places that occur when you move from one stage to another tend to be the most difficult places for most people, because you usually have no idea what is happening to you. St. John of the Cross wrote about one of these places when he discussed "the dark night of the soul." These times may seem dark, as you may feel lost and alone. There is a beautiful little book of letters written anonymously, probably by a fourteenth-century Christian monk, to a spiritual novice. The language is that of his time, and so we have to translate it to more contemporary thought, yet the monk's advice is direct and relevant for us. In this book, *The Cloud of Unknowing*, the monk describes those in-between places and says, in essence, that God puts you into these gray, befuddled places as an act of love, so that the Spirit may work on you and help you to transform. The monk's advice is to hang on to whatever bit of love you can find within yourself, and that will protect you and help you through this "lost" place until the sun shines again for you—when you have reached the next stage (Johnston 1973).

That is helpful advice for all of us. You may, if you wish, just change the language to whatever works for you, whether

God is a "she" or God becomes "the universe" or your own deepest self. The reality is that this process, this journey, seems to be universal, and you can learn from those who have gone before, even though you may conceptualize the process quite differently. Hanging on to whatever love you can find within, even though it may not seem like much, is a wonderful practice. Jan has had moments, long ago in difficult situations, when she thought there was no love anywhere, yet when she re-read the monk's words, she realized that indeed there *was* love, perhaps in her children's eyes, in a phrase in a Bach chorale, or in the kind gesture of a stranger at the grocery store.

Do I Need a Teacher?

The discussion of maps, paths, and journeys inevitably leads to the question, "Do I need a teacher?" The answer, once again, is, "It all depends." For many people, a spiritual teacher or guide is a tremendous help in getting through the hard places, in figuring out just where you are going and how you are going to get there—even though there is really no *place* to go, only a process of growth. For others, life itself becomes the teacher. While we have found that our spiritual teachers were critical to our own spiritual development, we are aware that times are changing. Reliable, knowledgeable, deep teachers are scarce, maybe more so than in the past, and we are in an era in which people are more reluctant to trust someone in such a role. While there are some excellent teachers available in some places, it is true that the teacher/guide role has been abused by many. Sometimes it is hard to distinguish a "real" teacher from a phony or one who takes advantage of the power of the role to use people. Some of the best simply call themselves "spiritual friends" and refuse to take on an authoritarian role.

Suppose you feel the need for a teacher to help you at a certain point. How might a teacher help you? A spiritual teacher, guide, or friend is someone who is willing and able to commit to a deep relationship with you in order to walk beside you on your journey. A good teacher/guide/friend will:

- Exhibit complete honesty and integrity.

- Have a harmonious personal atmosphere that "rings true."

- Find out what your spiritual situation and needs are.

- Help you find spiritual practices that work for you.

- Monitor your progress with regular face-to-face meetings (unless you live in different places, so that the phone or some other form of communication will be necessary).

- Respect your personal boundaries scrupulously.

- Be available (on the phone or in person) for consultation if you should experience a life crisis.

- Help you navigate the transition places between stages on your journey.

- Trust your own inner guidance and help you get in touch with it.

- Respect your own goals and your own sense of your life's purpose.

- Help you integrate your spiritual journey with your daily life so that you stay grounded and centered.

- Help you gain confidence in yourself and your judgment.

- Challenge you to take new and sometimes scary steps.

- Let you go when it is time for you to "graduate" from a period of more intensive guidance into independent practice.

It's also useful to know what a good teacher will not do, as there are several pitfalls. A *real* teacher will not:

- Make you dependent.

- Give you advice, except with regard to matters such as spiritual practices and avenues for spiritual progress.

- Violate your personal boundaries (e.g., absolutely no sexual advances, no requests for money except for reasonable workshop fees and such, and no requests for personal services).

- Present himself or herself as being "perfect." Teachers are imperfect humans, like all of us.

- Expect you to violate your own personal values and ethical principles.

- Expect you to change your life goals, unless you wish to do so.

The teacher-student relationship, should you decide to enter into one, should be a relationship of deep respect and trust on both sides. A real teacher makes herself vulnerable to a student, for she is sharing the deepest parts of herself with the student. The student must honor this trust and be careful not to hurt the teacher in any way. Likewise, if the student is to learn, the student must open up to the teacher, so that the teacher may see what practices will be most effective for that student. This relationship is so delicate that it requires both participants to have absolute integrity. It might be seen as a soul-to-soul relationship, a beautiful thing that lasts forever, long after the student has "graduated."

This discussion might leave you asking, "But is there really anyone like that in this world?" That is a reasonable question, as there are few such teachers available. If you decide that this is what you want, it would be wise to check with friends and knowledgeable people to make sure that the person you are considering is truly a *real* teacher. That said, there is an old saying: "When the student is ready, the teacher will appear." There is some truth to that. It is possible that there is someone near you who might serve as a teacher for you. Many real teachers live quietly and unassumingly, and they may hide their depths from the world in order to survive. They may not look like your conception of a spiritual teacher; they may, however, be willing to work with you.

Life as a Teacher

As we suggested at the beginning of this chapter, you may find that life itself is your most powerful teacher. Once you commit to a spiritual journey, you will find that everything that happens to you is a teaching: everyone you encounter may carry some sort of teaching, Nature may speak to you, and situations may reveal themselves to be teachings. There is nothing that is random, once you wake up to the pattern that exists under the surface of life. One can explain this phenomenon in a variety of different ways. Some say it is synchronicity, some suggest it is related to energy flow, and others may use astrology to explain the patterns. Some speak of God or saints or nature spirits or the Spirit of Guidance. Whatever the explanation, our experience is that life is a constant teacher. Sometimes the teachings are gentle, sometimes they are humorous, and sometimes they come with a wallop! Sometimes life opens totally unexpected doors that you hardly notice until someone or something calls your attention to them. At other times, life may close every door but one—and often that one open door may be one that you had been avoiding, but you will realize that this is the guidance of life helping you to focus.

Jan shares this example of listening to and learning from her life:

Recently, I was having trouble focusing on writing, even though I enjoy it. Previously made, compelling commitments were pulling me in what seemed like a thousand different directions. I told a friend that I felt as if I were trying to ride four wild horses at once, standing straddled between the middle two, hanging onto the reins of all four, and charging off like a circus rider. I was running from meeting to meeting, and many aspects of my life were not going as smoothly as usual. Does this sound familiar to you? A few mornings ago, I noticed that early-morning gardening, my greatest joy in the summer, felt empty. It didn't bring the great welling up of happiness in my heart that I usually feel when I tend the flowers, and I wondered what was wrong. Then it hit me that I really needed to put writing first this summer, no matter what. I dropped everything else for a couple of days to get the writing re-energized, and it flowed beautifully. When I went out to the garden a few mornings later for just a short time, the joy was back. I had finally figured it out, and life started working again. Life itself provided the lesson that I needed.

Connecting with the Web of Life— Nature as a Teacher

For many of us, Nature is the most amazing teacher possible. Being in the natural world lifts the spirit and provides guidance in totally unanticipated ways, usually through synchronicity, as Jan has found:

Hawks and eagles have spoken to some of my deepest questions at crossroads in my life. They have affirmed a decision to buy a piece of land by showing up and circling above it (when they were curiously absent from other pieces of land). Sometimes a powerful inner revelation has been underscored by the sudden, surprising appearance of an eagle overhead. Once it happened when I was driving to work down the quiet streets of the town where I teach. An unexpected understanding flashed through my mind, and then my eyes were somehow lifted to see a bald eagle gliding low over the street, just a few feet above my car. Never before or since have I seen an eagle in this town.

Twice when I have taken groups of students to visit the Pine Ridge Reservation of the Oglala Lakota Nation in South Dakota, we have been greeted at the outskirts of the reservation by a great golden eagle— sitting on the ground by the side of the road, as if he were just waiting to welcome us. As striking as that was, it wasn't quite so surprising, as golden eagles and other wildlife are abundant on the Pine Ridge Reservation, and all of life seems especially alive there.

Lessons from the natural world are daily gifts in such places as Native American reservations, but if we tune in everywhere, we will be blessed with a multitude of such gifts. We will pursue this topic more fully in chapter 13, "Connecting with Nature."

The Path of Love and Relationships

For many of us, the most powerful path is the path of love. Actually, love and life may be seen as the same thing, for life is created from love. The dwelling place of love on this earth is the human heart, and the more you open your heart to the force of love, the larger your heart will become. It is possible that your heart may expand and expand to the point at which it is capable of holding the entirety of humanity, the entire planet, the entire universe, and beyond. When you reach this point, you will become a fountain of love, and you will be transformed by the love flowing through you.

Chapter 16, "The Transformative Power of Relationships," will delve more deeply into the ways in which you may allow your relationships to help you grow spiritually.

How Do I Know If I'm Growing?

Monitoring your spiritual growth is a challenge, since none of us has the perspective to see our own self very clearly. Some friends, relatives, and coworkers may not see clearly either, as they may misunderstand the signs of spiritual growth and may even wish that you do not change, since this may threaten the comfort of your old ways of relating to one another.

How, then, can you know if you are unfolding spiritually? One of the most effective ways is to continue to work on increasing your awareness of yourself—your thoughts, actions, breath, intentions, and heart energy—from moment to moment. You don't want to become so introspective that you are unable to function in the world, though, as the kind of spirituality we affirm calls us to embrace others, but you may gradually learn to monitor yourself while you are doing other things, as well as while you are quiet. As you watch yourself, you may suddenly realize, "I am becoming more peaceful" or "I am less needy than I used to be." Sometimes a friend may give you feedback, such as, "It seems easier to get close to you now." These are the moments when you will realize that something is changing.

One of the most common signs of spiritual growth is that you may appear to be a bit softer, as the hard edges that all of us have to some degree will begin to melt. You may feel more relaxed, and you may find that you are living more fully in the present moment, with less anxiety about the future or the past. There are so many qualities that point to spiritual growth that we decided to make a list for you—but please do not use this list to create impossible expectations for yourself. It is meant to inspire you to notice the changes that are occurring in your being and in your life. This list is only a beginning, so you might like to create your own list.

Qualities Related to Spiritual Development
Being and Knowing Qualities

- Joyful
- Peaceful
- Centered
- Grounded

- Creative
- Aware
- Present in the moment
- Balanced, showing equanimity
- Self-confident
- Accepting of life
- Soft
- Focused
- Purposeful
- Free
- Humble
- Quiet inside, having inner stillness
- Nonjudgmental
- Less ego-involved
- Magnetic
- Flexible
- Clear
- Responsible
- Able to laugh at little things
- Able to laugh at self (not taking self too seriously)
- Appreciative of beauty
- Intentional, purposeful
- "Real"—you can be who you are
- Heart "coming alive"
- Tolerant of ambiguity, accepting of the "messiness" of life
- Understanding of complexity—the paradoxical nature of life
- Aware of emotions

- Mastery of self
- Not overly attached to material things

Relationship Qualities

- Harmonious
- Loving
- Kind, compassionate
- Connected
- Self-sufficient (not overly needy)
- Able to "give and take"
- Does not need others' constant approval
- Actions grounded in love
- Forgiving
- Accepting of others
- Nondefensive
- Generous
- Truthful
- Balance between attachment and detachment
- Open-minded
- Dependable
- "Tuned in" to others
- Difficulties handled with humor, when appropriate

These lists are a beginning; see where you go with them. You probably will resonate with some of the qualities and find that others seem a bit foreign to you. This is natural, as all of us have unique constellations of qualities that are evolving within us. You may have noticed that we did not include some of the qualities that you may associate with spiritual development, such as illumination, wisdom, and enlightenment. These develop gradually, usually when you least expect them, and chasing them can be counterproductive. If (or when) you do have extraordinary moments in which the universe seems to open up to you, your being is flooded with light, you feel one with all creation and all being, or you experience visions of other realities, it is usually best to hold that experience in your heart. It is a gift, and telling others about it may cause the beauty and power of the experience to diminish, in part because most people will not be able to comprehend your experience. The only persons we would suggest confiding in are your spiritual guides, persons who you know have integrity and who have had similar experiences.

four

The Spiritual
Architecture of the Self

Throughout this book and many others, you will see references to the human aura and to the energy centers, sometimes called *chakras*. We will give you a brief introduction to the aura and energy centers, although this subject is vast and too complex to include a thorough explanation within this short chapter. If you find our brief explanation of interest, we suggest that you pick up a book about auras and explore this fascinating topic in depth.

The human aura can be described as the combination of bodies that the divine spark of life (spirit), our essential being, has put on as it has entered manifestation. Your aura is the vibrational clothing needed to function on the various planes of existence. It lies between you as a physical person and the source from which you, a fragment of the One Spirit, have come. Your being may be seen to encompass several bodies, existing in layers surrounding your physical body in concentric circles. Starting with your physical body, each successive layer is related to a higher, more refined vibrational level. To function on a particular plane of existence (discussed below), you need to carry within you the vibrations of that plane.

Depending on their perspectives, writers have called these planes of existence by various names. Some have divided each plane into two or more subplanes. While this is a fascinating topic to explore deeply, we will look only at the broad outline and will use a mixture of terminology that we feel is useful and clear. The chart on the opposite page will give you a picture of the subtle bodies that the aura comprises, as well as a description of the plane of existence of which each is a part.

This chart gives you a synopsis of the seven planes of existence and the bodies that make up your aura. It is important to realize that through your aura, you touch all levels of reality; in your subtle bodies, you participate in the vastness of life.

Subtle Bodies and Planes of Existence

Subtle Body	Plane of Existence
Body of Unity—The part of us that is a part of the whole. The spirit within that is identical to the One Spirit.	*The Undivided Oneness*
Archetypal Body—The body of intelligence prior to consciousness. The vast potential of being is divided into archetypal potentialities.	*Archetypal Plane*—Plane of the archangels (or the vast categories of being that are beyond consciousness).
Spiritual Body—Body of the highest consciousness. Marked by consciousness of glory, exaltation, communion, and joy. The highest vibration of which consciousness can be aware. This is also the body that is involved in deep and abiding love.	*Spiritual Plane*—Plane of joy and exaltation. The plane that draws all life toward communion with the One. The plane of the highest consciousness and of deep love.
Mental Body—Body of thought, especially creative, noble, and discerning thought. Often divided between higher and lower thought.	*Mental Plane*—The plane of genius, of creative thought, of inspiration, and of understanding.
Astral or Emotional Body—Needs to be divided into higher and lower astral. The higher astral plane involves useful or inspiring emotional experiences. The lower astral involves degrading emotions such as greed, hate, and unchecked lust.	*Astral or Emotional Plane*—Higher astral is the realm of emotions. Lower astral is the realm that is evoked when talking about suffering in the afterlife. It is also the realm of demons and unhelpful disincarnate beings.
Etheric/Magnetic Body—The body in which the energy centers are anchored, although they can reach out into much higher levels of the aura. This is also the grayish, magnetic sheath that surrounds the body and can be seen fairly easily if you set your gaze at infinity.	*Etheric Plane*—The etheric plane serves as a bridge between the physical and nonphysical. Much spiritual healing uses the malleability of the etheric plane to affect the physical and subtle bodies.
Physical Body—The body with which you are most familiar.	*Physical Plane*—The plane where spirit has most fully become material.

The next point to realize is that your energy centers, or chakras, also relate to some extent to your subtle bodies and to the planes of existence. The illustration on the opposite page shows the position of your chakras. Related to the glands in your endocrine system, they are whirling vortexes anchored in your etheric body and extending into the appropriate subtle bodies.

Let's look at each energy center and see what it is associated with and how it affects our lives. While some centers may seem to be "higher" and more spiritual than others, ultimately they are all essential to being fully functioning, spiritually awake human beings. Rather than seeing some centers as being higher, it is more useful to see all of the centers as having the capacity for spiritual growth and development in the specific realms that they serve. Hence the root center, when transformed, can help to ground and incarnate our highest selves once we have contacted that aspect of ourselves through the higher centers.

- Root Center (*Muladhara Chakra* in Sanskrit): This center is located at the base of the spine (some say at the perineum) and is associated with your connection to earth and physical life, survival issues, and the "will to be" at its basic level. Its color is red. Positive aspects of this center relate to establishing a grounded sense of self. Unbalanced aspects relate to stubbornness, being stuck at the survival level of consciousness, gluttony, and hoarding.

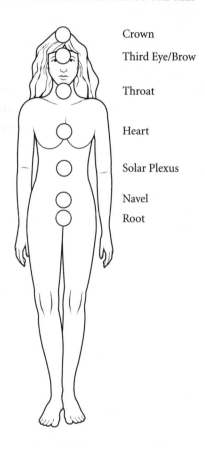

Crown

Third Eye/Brow

Throat

Heart

Solar Plexus

Navel

Root

- Navel Center (*Swadhisthana Chakra*): Located below the navel, this center is related to pleasure seeking, sexuality, and creativity in worldly activities. The color is orange. Its positive aspects involve the capacity to give and accept physical love and creativity in everyday life. Lack of balance can involve obsessive sexuality, repressed sexuality, and rigidity.

- Solar Plexus Center (*Manipura Chakra*): Located in the solar plexus, this center is related to your personal power. Its color is yellow. Positive aspects of this center involve assertiveness and the ability to make things happen for the better in our lives. Unbalanced use involves seeking excessive power and using power and domination unwisely.

- Heart Center (*Anahata Chakra*): This is located in the center of the chest. The heart is the first of the "higher centers" and is a very important center for spiritual development (refer to chapter 9, "Creating a Living Heart"). This center is seen as the place where the energies of the upper and lower centers meet. Its color is green, although a very beautiful pink may also be seen. The golden light of the sun is also related to the heart. Positive aspects of the heart center relate to love, compassion, and empathy, as well as other expanding qualities that make one larger and wiser. An unbalanced heart center may lead to sentimentality, possessiveness, and extreme vulnerability.

- Throat Center (*Vissudha Chakra*): Located in the throat, this center relates to communication, self-expression, higher creativity, and receiving and holding the gifts from the higher spheres. Its color is turquoise. Positive aspects of the throat center relate to speaking your truth as well as receiving and communicating inspiration. Unbalanced throat energy may involve rigid nonconformity and fanaticism on the one extreme and the inability to communicate your perspective on the other.

- The Third Eye—Brow Center (*Ajna Chakra*): The third eye is located between and slightly above the eyebrows. The color is seen as a deep indigo blue or violet. This center governs such characteristics as clarity, discernment, and wisdom. It is often called the wisdom center. The third eye also involves intuition and certain psychic abilities. The third eye tends to unmask the world around us and allows us to see what lies beneath the surface of life. The positives of this center relate to the development of insight and wisdom. An unbalanced third eye is related to the development of psychic abilities before their time, on one hand, and becoming an insufferable know-it-all, on the other.

- Crown Center (*Sahasrara Chakra*): The crown center is located at the top of the head and extends above. Its color is white or clear diamond light, although some see rainbow colors. It is related to transcendence and vastly expanded consciousness. Our connection with the divine realms, this center is the alpha and omega of our consciousness. From a positive point of view, the opening of the crown center leads to the experience of the unity of life. As such, it is the seat of the highest wisdom. It is also important as we connect with our purpose in life. An unbalanced crown center can be seen in spacey, ungrounded, or obsessive individuals.

While this rather straightforward list may seem easy to work with, the system appears more intricate as you develop more insight and knowledge. In actuality, the centers often work in tandem, as with the crown and third eye or the heart and the solar plexus. Some believe that there are fewer centers than seven, because they see these tandem centers as just two aspects of one center. Many people see energy centers extending above the crown, and there are also auxiliary centers throughout your body that work in conjunction with the major centers. For those starting out on a spiritual journey, these issues are of little consequence. The matter of primary importance is to become more aware of the nature of your own subtle self.

As you progress spiritually, your energy centers and aura change. Your energy centers wake up, clear out stuck energies, and begin to operate up to their potential. The predominant colors in your aura begin to change, reflecting the changes in your consciousness. These changes can be seen by those who have the psychic abilities (which may be learned), but more importantly, they may be felt by anyone with the sensitivity. In addition, there is a law of affinity in the universe: your vibrational level draws to you people and experiences that have an affinity with the energy of your being.

EXERCISE: ENERGIZING YOUR AURA WITH LIGHT

1. Begin this exercise by becoming aware of your breath.

2. As you inhale, visualize a vortex of red light at the base of your spine, and as you exhale, visualize the red light

growing and becoming clearer, more vibrant and alive. Repeat this five times.

3. As you inhale, visualize a vortex of orange light just below your navel. As you exhale, visualize the orange light growing and becoming clearer, more vibrant and alive. Repeat five times.

4. As you inhale, visualize a vortex of yellow light at your solar plexus. As you exhale, visualize the yellow light growing and becoming clearer, more vibrant and alive. Repeat five times.

5. As you inhale, visualize a vortex of green light at the center of your chest. As you exhale, visualize the green light growing and becoming clearer, more vibrant and alive. Repeat five times.

6. As you inhale, visualize a vortex of turquoise blue light in your throat. As you exhale, visualize the light growing and becoming clearer, more vibrant and alive. Repeat five times.

7. As you inhale, visualize a vortex of indigo blue or vio-let light between and slightly above your eyebrows. As you exhale, visualize the light growing and becoming clearer, more vibrant and alive. Repeat five times.

8. As you inhale, visualize a vortex of clear diamond or white light at the top of your head and extending above it. As you exhale, visualize the light growing and becoming clearer, more vibrant and alive. Repeat five times.

9. Finally, as you inhale, visualize that you are drawing energy from the earth up through the base of your spine, energizing the vortexes of the first three centers while at the same time drawing celestial energy down through the crown and energizing the top four vortexes. While exhaling, visualize the respective colors radiating forward from each center into infinity, fueled by the telluric and celestial energies that are flowing into your subtle bodies. Repeat five times.

After you finish this exercise, you may sit quietly for a few minutes and enjoy the feeling of being fully awake, energized, and aware of the energies in your being.

five

Spiritual Practices

You may have heard people refer to spiritual practices and wondered exactly what that meant. Generally, the idea is that spiritual practices are like physical exercises—but instead of tuning up your physical body, they tune up your spiritual being. A bonus is that they may benefit your body as well, since the physical and spiritual bodies interpenetrate in intricate ways. We will discuss various spiritual practices that have the potential to help you develop your spiritual capabilities and thus will speed up your development. Some of the practices that we will suggest have been around for hundreds of years and have been tested by many people. Others have been developed relatively recently. We have tested all of them to make sure that they are effective and safe. Practices, however, affect each person differently, and some people are more prepared than others to handle the powerful transformative energies that some practices may evoke, so use your own judgment. Check your intuition, and use the practices that feel right for you.

In this chapter, we will discuss various types of spiritual practices; you will also have an opportunity to go deeper with these practices, as they are used as exercises following most chapters throughout this book. Most of these spiritual practices use a device like breath, light, sound, or visualization to focus your mind and accomplish your purpose. Many fall within the category that most people call meditation, but in reality, they also facilitate other forms of spiritual work, such as prayer, healing, and creative imagination.

Practices Using the Breath

One of the most basic processes in life is the simple inhalation and exhalation of breath, yet this fundamental reality is the foundation of many profound spiritual practices. Breath has long been one of the great secrets of life, because it is more than the process of inhalation and exhalation. The breath itself carries powerful life-giving, healing energies.

Many ancient languages use the same word to refer to both breath and spirit, and there is a reason for that. Breath is both spirit and life. It serves as the intermediary between the world of spirit and our physical life. For these reasons, breathing is a foundation upon which we can build spiritual practice; the condition of our breath reflects the condition of our being. You might want to check right now and observe whether your breath is shallow or deep, fast or slow, steady or irregular. This sort of simple observation is a beginning for work with the breath. Generally, when you observe your breath, it will start to slow down and become more regular.

There are several common ways to use breath for spiritual practice. One way is by doing specific practices designed to improve the quality of your breath. This use of breath involves techniques such as alternate nostril breathing, purification or cleansing breaths, and rhythmic breathing. These practices have the benefit of refining your aura, strengthening your connection with spiritual realms, and centering your consciousness, as well as quieting and grounding you in everyday life.

Another way to use your breath is as a swing into which you can put certain thoughts. You may use the natural rhythm created by inhaling and exhaling to anchor the two sides of a thought. For instance, as you inhale, you feel yourself centered in the here and now, and as you exhale, you feel yourself reaching out for guidance from spiritual realms. There are many paired thoughts such as these that can be made part of your "breath swing."

Simply concentrating on your inhalation and exhalation and clearing your mind of all else is a classic breathing exercise. This exercise, which is at the basis of much spiritual practice, is not only very useful in itself, but it can serve as a sort of default mode to which you can return no matter what other technique you are using. You may notice that the more you try to clear your mind to concentrate on the breath, the more extraneous thoughts enter your mind.

Don't be concerned—this is normal! Rather than fighting the thoughts, just observe them, let them go, and then return to your concentration on the breath. When this happens, you may feel comforted to know that this is so common that it has been given a name. Congratulations, you have met the "monkey mind," the part of your mind that never wants to be quiet. If you fight the thoughts, they may get stronger, but if you gently observe and release them, they will gradually subside. A little humor also helps. When a thought comes racing through, you may simply smile inwardly and think, "Oh, there goes that thought again," and return to the breath. Being gentle with yourself is generally the best approach, as spiritual practices are about unfolding and growing, not about whipping yourself into shape.

Exercise: Rhythmic Breathing

You may use this rhythmic-breathing exercise as a baseline for other breathing practices. Inhale for the length of four heartbeats and then exhale for the length of four heartbeats. Whenever you become aware of your breathing, gently bring the rhythm back to this four-four count. In addition to helping you notice your breath, this practice will also help to bring balance into your life. It is particularly pleasant to do this practice while walking in a garden—or even on city streets, if you are able to maintain your awareness. You may coordinate your breath with your steps, and you will find that you have begun a wonderful walking meditation practice.

Practices Using Light

Practices with light tend to be lovely, uplifting practices that make you feel joyful. They have the power to purify your aura, energize you, and make you more radiant. Practices with light involve visualization of light, usually in relationship to your own body or subtle bodies. The power of working with light relates to the fact that we are beings of light, even though we sometimes forget our light and the light of which we are a part. When beginning our work with light, it is helpful to think of ourselves as pieces of the all-pervading light that have traveled far from their source. By working with light, we begin to remember our connection with the One Light that connects all of us. This Light has been called "celestial light," "white light," the "uncreated light," the "all-pervading light," the "Light of the Divine," and the "Light of Divine Intelligence." Whatever one calls it, this is a brilliant light that is seen inwardly.

When working with this all-pervading light, you might start by picturing white or clear diamond light filling your head, your heart, and your entire body and extending beyond. You might also visualize yourself as a being of light living in a sea of light. Most people need to work with light intensively for a time before they glimpse this wonderful light, but you may be rewarded with such an experience when you least expect it. Going on a spiritual retreat where you have time to concentrate on light practices for days at a time helps greatly, but regular practice every day also will lead to increasing realization of your inner light as a part of the great sea of all-pervading light.

You may work with light to purify, change, and develop the capacities of your subtle bodies, as we discussed in chapter 4, "The Spiritual Architecture of the Self." In a way, working with light is like working with clay, as you are working with a malleable substance that can be transformed into something beautiful. For this reason, spiritual practices that involve working with light may act as helpful tools in the transformation work of spiritual development. We might add that working with light practices leads to great joy. If you, like most people, have a tendency to feel down or even get depressed from time to time, working with light is one of the best and quickest ways to lift your spirits. We don't say, "Lighten up!" to each other for nothing!

Finally, we need to remember another aspect of working with light, which is using light to purify and brighten up your aura. This work is another way to clean out your emotions and the field of energy that surrounds you. We recommend returning to chapter 4 from time to time for the practices that deal with the light of your aura.

EXERCISE: BREATHING LIGHT

This exercise combines breathing and light practices to awaken and enhance your experience of the higher energy centers in your body. Take a moment and imagine that as you inhale, you draw a clear diamond light from above your head down through the crown chakra at the top of your skull. As the light reaches the pineal gland at the center of your head, directly behind your eyes, refract the light forward as you exhale, so that it becomes an indigo blue that projects from your third eye, between your eyebrows. It becomes a sky blue light as it projects through your physical eyes. At the same time, the diamond light from above your head also reaches your heart chakra in the center of your chest, where it projects in all directions like a golden sun. Repeat this breath until it becomes easy to visualize. As you become more accustomed to the exercise, these energy centers will feel increasingly alive and radiant, and you will gradually notice an enhancement of the qualities associated with the centers. For example, you may find that your intuition becomes clearer and that your heart feels more compassionate.

Practices Using Sound

Sound practices may be directed toward various parts of your spiritual body, such as specific energy centers. Sound is vibration, and there is a long history of using sound to influence consciousness by refining, energizing, and healing our subtle bodies. Because sound can convey meaning, many sound practices are also designed to change the typical thoughts that we carry with us. Let's look at these uses of sound more closely.

There are certain sounds that have beneficial effects on a person, whether they contain conscious meaning or not. For instance, a good Tibetan bell produces a sublime sound with no overt meaning, yet when you sound the bell, it may elevate your consciousness almost immediately. How does this happen? The complete answer would require another book, but the short answer is that it is the *overtones* of a well-made Tibetan bell that create their amazing effect on the consciousness. (Overtones are the subtle harmonic tones you may hear resonating above the notes that are sung or played on an instrument.) Learning to produce overtones as you sing or chant, in fact, is the key to the most effective sound practices. It takes practice, but virtually anyone can do it. Perhaps you have been lucky enough to hear a recording of some of the singers from Mongolia who are able to produce an incredible range of overtones simply by using their voices as instruments. We've been fortunate to hear such singers in person; they told us that their tradition says that the original singers learned to make their complex, rich sounds by sitting next to waterfalls in the Mongolian countryside and listening to the water's overtones.

The sound "aah" is another example of the impact of sound practices. If you say a word that emphasizes the "aah" sound, such as *God*, *hallelujah*, or *Allah*, it will have a beneficial effect on the heart chakra. Why? The short answer is that the "aah" sound resonates in the heart center. After a little practice, you may find that you can actually feel your heart center revivifying as you sing or chant a word or phrase using this sound. You might like to know that even simple singing, without any particular emphasis on sounds, tends to open the heart—as long as your song is harmonious and has upbeat lyrics.

Using certain sounds focuses the vibrations on specific chakras and may speed up your development. Sounds used in this way are sacred to their traditions and need to be used in a respectful, meditative context. The "om" sound, as in the Buddhist and Hindu "Om," tends to resonate in the crown center. It is understood as the underlying sound of the entire universe, and when chanted, it may lead to the consciousness of universal Oneness. The "Hu" sound for Sufis is the natural name for the Supreme Being, the beginning of sound and the culmination of all sounds. This sound especially relates to the throat chakra (the "oo" activates the throat center), but it is so all-pervading that it enhances the crown and the heart centers as well. Repeating the "Hu" sound with a focus on the heart center is an example of the use of this sacred sound, in this case to open, purify, and heal the heart. Placing the "Hu" in the throat center makes one more receptive to beautiful, immense realms of spiritual guidance and support. A word of caution is needed here: some sounds, such as "Om" and "Hu," tend to make your consciousness vast and may result in your feeling "spacey," so they should be used only when you are in a protected meditative situation—never when driving a car or doing anything else that requires your full attention. Sounds such as these, which work on the higher energy centers, need to be balanced with other sound practices or other spiritual practices that will ground you.

Repetition of a word or phrase that has a profound spiritual meaning has been an important part of spiritual practices throughout the world. Whether we refer to the repetition as mantra, *wasifa*, words of power, chanting, or prayer, we are addressing the use of the vibration and meaning of a word or phrase for the purposes of spiritual development.

In the East, it is said that the quickest way to enlightenment is by singing or repeating one of the many sacred names of God.

Jan remembers being part of a spiritual group sitting with the venerable Hindu teacher Baba Sita Ramdas Oncarnath:

> Traveling with Pir Vilayat Inayat Khan, our group had been visiting holy places and teachers of several spiritual paths in northern India, and we were in New Delhi at the time of a solar eclipse, an event that people in India took quite seriously. We spent four hours during the eclipse sitting in meditation with Baba Sita, a tiny, ancient, frail-appearing man with long white hair wrapped around and around his head, like a crown of dreadlocks. His energy was anything but frail. After struggling to sit still—this was before I had managed to get the body calmed down—I suddenly felt an immense power in my heart center. It was actually almost like a physical blow, as if my heart were being blasted open and filled with immense energy. After that, it was easy to sit in blissful silence for the remainder of the time. When the session was over, Baba Sita opened his sparkling eyes, smiled delightedly, and talked directly to us, just like a kindly, wise old friend. Do you know what his first words were? He pointed emphatically at us and said, "*Nam, Nam!*" ("The Name, the Name!"). Then he switched to English. "You know, the most important thing you can do is to repeat the name of God. Just say it, again and

again, and you will be transformed!" He was li
proof of the power of sound practices.

EXERCISE: PRACTICES WITH SOUND

While there are countless words in many languages that
you may use as sound practices, we will give you a few
phrases to begin your practice. Many of these phrases use
words that emphasize various chakra-opening sounds,
such as the "aah," the "ee," and the "oh" sounds. Many
carry deep meaning that has been intensified by use over
the centuries. We have purposefully selected phrases from
various traditions so that you can choose those with which
you feel most comfortable.

- *"Lord Jesus Christ, have mercy on me."* This is a version of the "Jesus Prayer" used by the early Christian
  desert fathers—and perhaps by a few intrepid "desert
  mothers" as well. It is a practice intended to help one
  "pray without ceasing," to facilitate the remembrance
  of the Christ within and without.

- *"Om Sri Ram, Jai Ram, Jai Jai Ram."* (Pronounced
  "ohm shree rahm, jay rahm, jay jay rahm.") This
  phrase is the Hindu practice of Ramnam, most nota-
  bly taught by Papa Ramdas and Mother Krishnabai.
  Literally meaning "Victory to Ram," it strengthens
  and opens the heart.

- *"Gate, Gate, Paragate, Parasamgate, Bodhi Svaha."*
  (Pronounced "gah-tay, gah-tay, para-gah-tay, para-
  sahm-gah-tay, boh-dee svah-ha.") The mantra at the

end of the Buddhist Heart Sutra, this phrase means, paraphrased, "Gone, gone, gone beyond, gone beyond the beyond, awakening." In our experience, this phrase lifts one beyond the limitations of time and space, yet it also keeps one centered in the heart.

- "*Ishk Allah m'abud lillah.*" (Pronounced "ishk allah mah-bood lee-lah.") The Sufi *dhikr* (remembrance) of love, this practice means, in essence, "God is Love, Lover, and Beloved," and it takes one into the vast ocean of all-encompassing Love.

- "*I am the eyes of God.*" This practice takes one to a high state of being where one sees from the divine perspective.

If you find that you "resonate" with sound practices, you may wish to try others. Richard's previous book, *Authentic Spirituality,* contains additional words to use in your practice. Sound practices are powerful tools, so if you wish to delve more deeply into this realm, we strongly recommend that you find an experienced teacher who understands such practices. Sound practices need to be selected carefully so that they work with specific qualities that you need to develop. Should you pick a practice that reinforces a quality that is already strong in your personality, you might create an unbalanced state that could lead to unfortunate results. Even the number of times you repeat a practice matters, as does the pronunciation of the words. With careful guidance, you will find that sound practices are an unparalleled way to enhance your spiritual development.

Visualization

Many spiritual practices involve visualization of some sort. Visualization can be mixed with breathing and sound practices and is obviously the primary method when working with light. Visualization may be mixed with meditation. (We will discuss the various forms of meditation in chapter 11, "Meditation.")

Visualization involves the use of your imagination to create mental images. Imagination can become quite real; the world of our imagination is a special and misunderstood world. We tap into this creative world of imagination when we purposefully use the technique of visualization, which is quite different from fantasy. Fantasy is a random, nonpurposeful flow of images and ideas, or it may be an intentional flow of images for noncreative purposes. Creative imagination, which we discuss several times from different perspectives throughout this book, is an activation of the inner world of the mind. This world has a reality of its own and can have a profound effect on you. Through purposeful visualization, you can significantly change your consciousness.

Use of creative imagination is not only an important way to develop spiritually, but it is also the world in which healers, shamans, visionaries, and spiritual teachers do much of their work. Much that is misunderstood in religious, spiritual, and mystical writings involves the assumption that descriptions and events necessarily all took place in the physical world. Those who have in the past attempted to share deep spiritual realities often have blended inner and outer events to create a picture of the rich tapestry of reality, which is so much larger and all-encompassing than we generally realize.

Exercise: A Visualization Exercise Using Light

The next time you are talking to a friend or loved one, try the following visualization:

1. Before you initiate the conversation, take a few seconds to imagine the light practice that you did earlier in this chapter. (Imagine a diamond light descending through your crown and then radiating from your eyes, third eye, and heart.)

2. While talking with your friend or loved one, try to keep the visualization of light going.

3. Visualize the person you are talking to as a being of light as well. See that person radiating brilliant light.

You may be surprised by the impact of this visualization, as you probably will almost literally see your friend or loved one "in a new light"! Not only do we often fail to see our own light, but we may also not observe the light that shines from others. These sorts of visualizations may help you to see more clearly the potential beauty in your fellow humans, as well as in yourself, and they may help you to connect more strongly with others. As a result, you will begin to feel happier and more at home in the world.

Practices for the Mind

It would require several very long books to begin to mention all of the different types of spiritual practices used around the world. What we have tried to do in this chapter is to give you a brief glimpse of several of the most widely used methods of spiritual practice. We will finish the chapter by mentioning a broad category of practices that are used to quiet, change, and broaden the mind and to keep it occupied while the work of spiritual development is going on.

Mindfulness

The practice of mindfulness has received considerable attention recently, with reason, as it is one of the most important practices for taming your mind. Our minds tend to be reluctant to let go of what they believe to be their rightful role: that of master. As you develop spiritually, it is your higher will that must become the master; your mind then relinquishes control but becomes a valued servant. To bring the mind around to this point of view, it is helpful to use techniques designed to harness the capacity of your mind while asserting the mastery of the higher will. What is this "higher will"? It comes from the power of the awakened heart, which is attuned to a universal, loving consciousness that is available to guide us throughout our lives. As you gradually clear your being of old baggage and allow new light and energy to awaken within, you will find yourself consulting your heart more often as you make decisions.

Out of this process emerges something new: your higher will.

Mindfulness involves developing mastery over your everyday habitual patterns of thinking and doing by focusing on the moment and the choice that is involved in each thought, activity, and feeling. This involves staying present in the moment—thinking before doing. It also usually involves inserting a spiritual practice into the space where habitual patterns might take over. Practicing awareness of each breath and repeating a sacred word or phrase inwardly are helpful ways to interfere with the old patterns. (Please refer to chapter 10, "Developing Mastery," for a more complete discussion of this process.)

Reading

We have known people who saw reading as their primary means of spiritual development. Although reading can take you only so far, it is understandable that some people feel this way at points along the path. If you have been searching for a while, you probably have run into certain books at what seemed to be exactly the right time. Not only that, but you may also have noticed that sometimes a book that you have shelved for a couple of years surprisingly comes alive for you. Maybe you couldn't get into that book right away, and then later, when you were ready, that same book opened its secrets to you in an almost magical way.

Finding the right book at the right time involves synchronicity and intuition; these factors get stronger as you progress along the path. It has been our experience that through some meaningful coincidence (synchronicity) or the experience of a book "reaching out" and saying "read me" (intuition), we have found a book or article that gives us a clue to the next step in our path.

The important thing to remember is that a book can only point in the direction. You must walk the path, and sometimes that takes help that is more personal and tailored to you specifically. A book cannot provide the spiritual transmission that comes from working with a guide or group. That which is silently passed from heart to heart is far more important in spiritual development than any knowledge that you might gain, although the knowledge is also necessary.

Mental Tasks

Sometimes in order to keep your mind from rebelling against its ultimate taming by your higher will, a teacher will give you a task to keep your mind busy while the real work is happening. Pir Vilayat Inayat Khan, our mentor and initiator into Sufism, would often talk to groups for long periods of time about deep esoteric topics and then tell us that the talking served mostly to occupy our minds so that the real work in our hearts could occur.

Zen teachers have used insoluble questions, called *koans*, to keep their students' minds busy while the work of enlightenment was happening. These questions, of which "What is the sound of one hand clapping?" is a classic example, serve the purpose of appeasing the student's mind by giving it a challenging task and forcing it to think outside of the box. Ramana Maharshi, a compassionate and incisive Hindu teacher, used to answer his students' questions by asking them, "Who is it that is asking?" This answer served as a spur to change the direction of their thinking, from concentrating on answers "out there" to looking for meaning within. Hazrat Inayat Khan used a similar approach when he said, "Look for the answer that uproots the question." This last statement has stopped us in our tracks more times than we can count—the impact has turned our minds inside out and, from time to time, has resulted in a great "aha!" experience.

Exercise: A Short Mind-Twister

All you need to do for this exercise is to ask yourself this question: "Who is it that is reading this book?"

Remember, whatever answer you give will serve to send you deeper to find out who *you* really are. No answer is correct, and the answer may change from moment to moment. A different answer may be needed to send you deeper at each step of the way.

As we have noted previously, there are hundreds of spiritual practices, many of which defy classification using the categories we have discussed. The path of spiritual development is both universal and personal. The mixture that will become your path will depend on many factors, and fortunately, you only need to take the next step on your path. The universe does not reveal what will happen after that—none of us ever knows that for certain. Sometimes we have thought that perhaps this is the ultimate "cosmic joke," but then we realized that actually, this is perfect. The path always unfolds in its own time. The next chapter, "Getting High and Going Deep," will take you further into the world of methods for spiritual development.

six

Getting High
and Going Deep

Spiritual development is about both getting high and going deep. You may be more comfortable with one of these directions than the other; people are typically more familiar with either the heights or the depths. Since the ascendancy of the Western patriarchal religions, fewer of us are comfortable with spiritual activities that take us deep. We might be inclined to say that patriarchal religions and the spiritual schools that developed around them stress getting high, while indigenous traditions from around the world are more closely related to going deep. This would be, however, only partially true. It may be more accurate to say that any mature spirituality will involve a blend of these directions and apply them to everyday life, whether the approach has evolved from a patriarchal or an indigenous tradition. The difficulty is that most people have had far less access to practices for going deep since "sky-oriented" monotheistic religions have become the norm in Western societies.

For those of us who live in industrial societies in which the indigenous traditions of our lands have been systematically eradicated, it is sometimes difficult to know what "going deep" means. We have some understanding of what it means to get high (in the spiritual sense), as many of us have been raised in traditions in which we participated in prayers, singing, or chanting—activities that often take one high. Getting high involves changing your consciousness to a more refined level and often leads to developing perspective and wisdom. It may involve compassion, love, devotion, and ecstasy; these feelings and qualities also tend to pull you out of your daily quagmires and into a sense of transcendence. Getting high is just that—getting above the pressures, difficulties, fears, and desires of daily existence.

Getting high is also related to the location that our cultures have chosen for the abode of our supreme beings. You have probably been told that God is situated in the heavens and that heaven is "up there" somewhere. If you believe that the Divine Being is up there, you pray, meditate, and do other forms of spiritual practice with the intention of "reaching up" or "elevating" your consciousness. "Up" has become associated with heaven, transcendence, and good. "Down," in contrast, has become associated with hell, materialism, and evil. Yet from a spiritual perspective, this dichotomy is artificial and not very helpful. The metaphors of "up" and "down" can be misleading.

There is only "here," and "here" has layers of manifestation. "Deep" is one of those manifestations, and we will discuss this direction first, since it may be a greater challenge for most than "high."

What, then, do we mean when we talk about going deep? In general, going deep is about being rooted in place, experiencing spirit in Nature, reclaiming your unconscious processes, and strengthening your relationship with the unseen world that is not up there somewhere but is here and now. Going deep is about being fully human, having access to the fullness of your soul. This certainly includes what the Jungians have termed "the shadow." In the last century, Jungian theorists have become a bastion of thought about the deep, since traditional indigenous peoples, who often know more about going deep than the rest of us, have been relegated to either invisibility or misunderstanding. Only now are we beginning to rediscover many of the indigenous traditions that hold the secrets of the ages about going deep, and much of this material is so woven into native cultures that modern Western minds have difficulty accessing and grasping its essence. Jungian writings have preserved some of this deep knowledge in words that are more accessible.

There are time-tested methods for going deep. Jan has suggested that one primary practice of going deep might be called "mining the treasures within." The gradual deepening and developing of the best of our human qualities, particularly those that are latent (i.e., not yet manifested), in order to create beautiful, clear, and powerful personalities is what we mean by "mining the treasures within." Practices that are currently described as shamanic, such as journeying and healing, are related to going deep. Discovering and working with your emotions, especially your negative emotions, is part of the experience of going deep. In mythology, cultures often associate this process with darkness, nighttime, the moon, and going into the earth. Gandalf's battle with the Balrog in Tolkien's *Lord of the Rings* is a good example of this process. Remember that Gandalf's battle began in the depths and then went even deeper, and finally the wizard was reborn in the heights. You can learn much from Gandalf's experience.

The process of contacting and integrating your shadow (the unconscious parts of your mind) involves some of the deepest work that you can do. Learning to be intimately in touch with the energies (spirits) of the world around you also takes you deep, as it requires that you enter into the realms of feeling and intuiting, located in the depths of life. Let's look at each of these methods of going deep.

Mining the Treasures Within

As our spirituality deepens, we might begin to conceptualize the purpose of humans in creation as helping to bring the Divine into manifestation. In other words, our purpose in life is to live out our highest ideals. We have typically projected our highest ideals onto gods that we believe exist in an otherworldly heaven, and then we try to live up to those god-ideals in our earthly lives. Sometimes we also project our anger and our prejudices upon our gods, and then we have a god that holds grudges, has a gender, promotes hate, and endorses war. Such projections turn out to be toxic to the well-being of the world and to us personally and need to be released as ideals. Instead, we need to discover the life-giving, world-enhancing qualities that are attributed to the gods and begin to make these positive qualities real in our own lives.

How does this process work? It begins when you start to reclaim your positive projections by going within, finding your unacknowledged positive qualities, and bringing them into your conscious life. What might you find? Wisdom, compassion, mastery, clarity, gratitude, joy, magnanimity, and many other beautiful qualities lie latent within, waiting to be recognized and manifested in your personality. It is not a simple or quick process to transform your less-developed nature (what some call our "animal nature") into a deeply human personality, yet becoming fully human is the goal. It is a rare and beautiful experience to encounter a truly transformed, truly human personality. When a person goes deep and transforms his or her personality, it has a profound effect on the world, for there is a ripple effect, and that person's energy impacts many. It may seem easier to worship a god from afar and then go about struggling with your daily business than it is to strive to become your ideals and transform your life, yet it is possible to do this adventurous and satisfying work of transformation. We will say much more about this, since many of the practices for spiritual development that are discussed in subsequent chapters are designed to help you accomplish this great work.

Shamanic Spirituality

The term *shamanism* is useful for describing an array of spiritual practices used by indigenous peoples to maintain a relationship and connect with realms of inner reality, often for the purpose of healing. The word *shaman* is from the language of the Tungus people in Siberia (Harner 1990, 20) but has come to be used to describe any practitioner of traditional indigenous healing and spirituality. Shamanism generally involves entering into an altered state of consciousness and journeying (usually in the company of an inner-world helper) in order to discover what is needed to help someone with whom the shaman is working.

Shamans use creative imagination to interact with inner-world realities. As Richard has described in *Authentic Spirituality,* "Creative imagination is the capacity for human consciousness to imbue its creations with meaning, psychological power, and an existence in the mind world." A shamanic practitioner learns to traverse the otherworld, using a highly developed creative imagination and influencing both inner and outer realities through his or her interventions. In addition to healing, the purposes for this work may involve seeking knowledge or acquiring power.

Our modern world sees shamanism as a vestige of older superstitious societies with no usefulness for today, but this is a mistake. If shamanic practice had not been persecuted and eliminated from Western societies by patriarchal religions and had instead been allowed to grow and mature into the modern times, it could have provided a missing component to understanding our world. Scientific, rational thinking can describe the physical world quite well, but it is unable to comprehend the unseen realities that are the world of shamanic practice. Creative imagination can keep you in a relationship with a vibrant, alive, and very important world in which you are imbedded, even though most people are unaware of its existence. This is the part of the world you explore when going deep.

The Psychology of Going Deep

One of the most confusing and yet important aspects of spirituality is trying to understand the interplay between spirituality and psychology. Psychology seems to play a bigger role in carving out a deep and wise personality structure than it does in getting high. The psychology of going deep is different from the spiritual practice of "mining the treasures within," because it often involves dealing with roadblocks and hang-ups rather than the discovery of the beauty within. These hindrances often prevent us from being able to touch our depths. As a matter of fact, one of the pitfalls of sky-oriented spirituality is that people can easily engage in the "spiritual bypass" of the more nitty-gritty aspects of psychological life. When engaging in a spiritual bypass, we can become unbalanced and also project that which we cannot integrate onto the world around us.

Understanding, expressing, and mastering your emotions keeps you in contact with your roots. As getting high became the only acceptable spiritual direction, the emotions that keep us in touch with our depths generally were relegated to the forbidden world of the feminine. Along with women, indigenous peoples, dreams, and the unconscious, emotions were considered feminine and unreliable. Reason reigned supreme in the patriarchal world. Reason is very useful when dealing with thoughts, ideas, theories, and knowledge, but it is not all that useful when trying to understand the world of feelings. Feelings are a bit more unruly but can help us understand a great deal of our experience. Feelings keep us in touch with our depths.

Integrating the Shadow

A very specific issue related to our discussion of psychological development is integrating the shadow. In many ways, this task can also be seen as a specific instance of "mining the treasures within." What the Jungians have termed *shadow* is something that everyone expecting to grow spiritually or intellectually needs to understand. Your shadow may be thought of as the parts of your being of which you are unaware. The shadow is what you have repressed and do not see as part of yourself, and it is also the part of your potential that has never been actualized. From this perspective, your shadow can be the rage that you have repressed because you fear its explosive potential, just as it can be the spiritual exaltation that lies within, completely beyond your awareness. In both of these instances, it is likely that you will use psychological defenses to protect yourself from the knowledge of what lies in the depths of your being. The rage may be repressed and turn into depression, whereas the exaltation may be projected onto a religious authority whom you then see as holy.

Going deep will require you to confront your shadow and integrate as much of it as you possibly can. It is common that at crucial times in your spiritual development you will be confronted by shadow material. It often arises symbolically or is seen in dreams, or, as we have already noted, it may be projected onto others. When it is time for people to confront their own inner shadows, some begin to see the shadow projected onto others around them. They may even feel that they are under psychic attack by others and may try to learn how to protect themselves. This is the sort of situation in which people need skilled spiritual guides who can help them to sort out their experiences and separate the shadow projections from reality.

The important work here is to learn to accept and own your inner anger, turmoil, and other disowned emotions so that you can move on to other spiritual work. At other times, it is necessary to accept and own your own spiritual depth and not project it onto spiritual teachers. This process, too, is difficult, because you may feel the need to distance yourself from beloved teachers for a time in order to find the depths of your own spiritual power.

Shadow issues like the ones we have just described may stand like closed portals on your path. They bar your way until you learn the keys to opening them, at which time entire new worlds appear before you. When you do not understand their nature, the depths are closed to you, and you have no choice but simply to take the unbalanced "high" path of a spiritual bypass. This may block true spiritual growth for a long time, until something powerful makes you take a second look at what you are avoiding in the deep places of your own being.

Natural Energies

The earth and the energies of Nature are very powerful, and even without the shamanic training that we discussed earlier, you can touch them through learning from Nature. Everything around you is alive with inner realities that are not apparent until you begin to open your consciousness to nonphysical realms. That inner, nonphysical world is more available when you are either in a natural environment or an environment dominated by an indigenous perspective. (You will find more on this in a later chapter.)

Synchronicity, the experience of meaningful coincidence, seems much more active when you are in a spontaneous, unplanned, natural environment. Events will often happen that shed light on your life's circumstances or a particular question you have. If you learn to listen to your environment and recognize synchronistic events, you may receive much-needed guidance from Nature.

As you advance along the path, or if you are by temperament a more psychic individual, you will begin to become aware of the consciousness in the natural world. You may become aware of energies that have been called *devas*, nature spirits, faeries, and hundreds of other names in other cultures. Primary cultures that we know of generally have lore about the "little people" who inhabit their lands. Many cultures also describe unseen beings that can help when called upon. Most indigenous cultures attribute some sort of consciousness to groupings of flora and fauna as well as to specific remarkable examples. Recently, Richard had an experience while sitting under an ancient cottonwood tree in New Mexico:

> I became aware of how much the tree had experienced and how much it could teach me, if I would only take the time to listen. I took some time, and the lessons it offered were remarkable. One phrase that has remained with me since that moment is "ancient but not old," which was a lesson for me about the proper occupation of old age. It speaks to me about learning how to bring patience and timeless wisdom into life without needing to lose spontaneity and joy.

The land upon which we live in eastern Nebraska was in past centuries occupied by the people of the Omaha Nation, the ancestors of some of our friends. There is wonderful energy in the woods, especially near a deep ravine, the spring-fed stream that flows through it, and a little hidden spring, the kinds of places where traditional peoples of many regions have found Nature energies or spirits. Whenever we visit these places, we feel invigorated, refreshed, and inspired by these energies, and we recommit to doing our best to work in harmony with them, learn from them, and protect them. The natural world around us is teeming with life. When we develop relationships with more parts of our environment, our lives may be enriched with new understandings of ancient realities.

Getting High

Getting high generally encourages perspective and transcendence and stresses an attunement to transcendent realities, that which we conceptualize to be above rather than within or below. Religious practices such as prayer, devotion, and worship are related to this perspective, which runs the gamut from a literalistic resignation to God's will to a deeper understanding of the alignment of the individual will with the divine intention. When not balanced by deep inner work, this approach may accentuate the separateness of God and humans and ask you to trust in an inaccessible higher power. One common path of transcendence is that of "loving God." When following this path, sometimes called *bhakti* (a Sanskrit word for "devotion"), the activity of loving draws your consciousness closer to the divine ideal and opens your personality to the possibility of spiritual development. Many schools of spiritual development use this practice, loving God, as a powerful way to elevate consciousness.

Meditation is not a significant part of many Western religions, except in Christian monasticism, but it is quite common in the East, where meditation is a central activity of most mystical schools of development. Meditation includes training your mind so that you may avoid being captured by day-to-day issues and can remain fixed on the ultimate goal. It may be otherworldly; some may use it as an attempt to avoid the exigencies of life in the world almost completely, as in monastic life or in living the life of a hermit. Meditation may also be a way to avoid the brain-washing of modern life, instead allowing you to keep your core focus on developing a loving and clear consciousness. Since it is such a huge topic, we will discuss meditation in a separate chapter.

We will touch on many more aspects of the spiritual activity of getting high later in this book. What is important to realize at this point is that if you are seeking spiritual development, you need to recognize that there will need to be more than one direction to your work. You will need to plumb the depths of your psyche and the world around you while at the same time seeking a vaster perspective. Those of us who inhabit the modern world often carry some bias regarding these directions. You may have grown up hearing that indigenous traditions were evil, backward, barbaric, or some other appellation, and therefore you may be skeptical about anything that relates to "Nature religion." You may have been so wounded or alienated by patriarchal religions that you either avoid religion altogether or will entertain only a path devoid of any "sky-god" trappings. The difficulty with both of these stances is that they relegate you to rejecting half of your potential path until you become capable of embracing the unity of life.

Spirituality and Everyday Life

This discussion of getting high and going deep requires taking a moment to consider actions in the middle range of everyday life. You might wish to ask yourself a few questions: To what extent do I align my actions with my level of realization? Do I usually treat those around me with kindness and compassion? Do I live up to my ideals most of the time? These are the tough but important questions that every spiritual aspirant needs to ask. True spiritual realization informs all of your relationships and actions. For most people, this happens gradually, as you struggle to bring your actions in the world in line with your realizations.

The most obvious sign of spiritual bypass is when a person who claims to love God is unable to love her or his neighbor. Self-delusion is common among seekers of Truth, and the clearest means of rooting out the kinds of delusion that all of us have is to demand that your life reflect your level of realization. If you discover that it doesn't, it is time to think about going back to the drawing board, as daunting as that might sound. There is nothing mysterious about spiritual development; it can be seen by those around you through your actions.

Please do not be too hard on yourself, however, if you feel that you fail to live up to your own expectations. Our experience is that many people expect too much of themselves and beat themselves up for their perceived failures. Spiritual development is not about a race to perfection; it is about opening yourself up to the grace of the universe and the beauty of the moment. True, you need to do some inner work as part of the journey, but ultimately, relaxing into the Oneness and living in the moment it bestows is what it is all about.

Everyday life is the place where we learn and apply the fruits of our spiritual development. Going deep and getting high are methods, but life is the place where it happens. Life cannot be escaped by becoming spiritual. Instead, your life is enriched immeasurably through the work of spiritual development. We will discuss this more fully in the final chapter.

EXERCISE: JOURNEYING

The most common form of shamanic practice is called *journeying*. When you journey, you enter non-ordinary reality through the use of creative imagination. The journeying process is often aided by rhythmic drumming or the use of a rattle. The following steps will give you a brief introduction to entering non-ordinary reality, or what we might also call "the deeper spaces of reality." This practice may help you to get in touch with symbolic aspects of your own being that you may not have experienced before, and eventually it may increase both your understanding and your vitality. If this exercise seems to evoke an apprehension of entering deep spaces, do not feel that you need to try it. You may find that after doing some psychological work in the depths, journeying will feel more comfortable. For others, this may be a delightful excursion into a symbolic world that is waiting to reveal itself to you.

- If you are with several people, have one person create a steady, moderate rhythmic beat with a drum or a rattle. If you are alone, put a drumming tape or CD in your stereo system. (They may be purchased through the Foundation for Shamanic Studies.) If you have neither a drum nor a tape available, you may do this practice as a meditation.

- Lie in a prone position on the floor, using a small pillow to support your head. Allow yourself to become very relaxed and quiet. Then imagine an entrance to the earth, like a hole, cave, canyon, or depression of some sort (probably one that you have seen and with which you are familiar).

- Now drop into that entrance and follow it until it takes you to the "lower world." This world will look a lot like the natural world with which you are familiar, but because it is an inner world, you will find that it can be magical.

- Explore this world for a while. Learn about its landscape, its flora and fauna. If you are struck by something special or magical, explore it and find its meaning for you.

- If you encounter in the inner world an animal of some sort, whether it be a mammal or bird, pay attention to it. If it reveals itself to you four times (either by appearing four different times or by showing you four sides or poses), it is there for you, and you can develop a relationship with this creature. It may become your power animal for a brief period of time, or for a lifetime. Power animals are an incredible blessing, for there is no end to the possibilities when working with a power animal.

- When you are finished exploring the "lower world," simply exit by the same means you entered. You will then return to ordinary reality.

After your journey, you will find it helpful to "process" your experience by writing about it in a journal or sharing the story with someone who understands shamanic journeying. They should be able to help you to interpret the meaning of the experience and will encourage you to find ways to apply what you have learned to your daily life. If you encountered a bird or animal during your journey, think about what this bird or animal might symbolize for you. You might be surprised by what you encounter. It might carry symbolic teachings for you, as such beings often embody qualities that you could bring to life to help you live more fully and effectively.

seven

Taming the Wanting Beast

As we implied in previous chapters, spiritual development is about *being* rather than striving. The idea of "working on" your spiritual development may be seen as a contradiction, although it might be better to look at this as a paradox. We need to put energy into our practices and our goals for change, yet we also need to let go and trust that the process of growth will unfold. Letting go and trusting are often difficult in contemporary Western societies. We are taught that to be worthy we must work hard, that we must be aggressive or at least assertive in order to succeed, and that our success is generally measured by how many of life's material things we are able to acquire. The rhythm of life, the rush to acquire more things, is fast, zooming along so quickly that we get caught up in the out-of-control pace. This is where the "wanting beast" kicks in. The wanting beast, that insatiable desire for more, is a primary barrier to being. Many of us spend an inordinate amount of time wanting more and more things, and we often forget that we are cogs in the wheels of modern capitalist economies that are built upon promoting an unquenchable appetite on the part of consumers—us. The catch is that the lifestyle that keeps contemporary economies booming also channels most of our energy away from spiritual development. It's hard to concentrate on *being* when social forces push us into *doing* more and more and more.

One of the first steps in becoming a spiritual person is to decide what you really want. What is your deepest heart's desire? This question will become an ongoing, integral part of your path. If you decide that your primary desire is to become wiser, more conscious, and more aware—in other words, more spiritual—then you will have established a priority against which other desires can be measured. You will also be connecting with your deepest inner purpose, which, if you are reading this book, is probably related to seeking awakening and illumination, as well as becoming a more authentic human being. It is hard to keep these goals in focus when everything around you says, "Work harder, earn more money, buy more things!" It is not unusual to find that your inner monologue, your moment-to-moment thoughts, become fixated on wanting, whether it is material things, emotional or psychological things, or mental or sometimes even spiritual things. When that happens, it is helpful to return to your primary desire and to weigh your wants against your deepest heart's desire. You may then decide whether it is the wanting beast that is plaguing you or whether a deeper desire is motivating you to grow.

Some mistake this battle with the wanting beast for the spiritual process of renunciation. There is a big difference. As we suggested earlier, the wanting beast refers to a habitual tendency that is programmed from childhood into those who grow up in modern industrialized economies. It is the habitual, unthinking, sometimes obsessive quality of the wanting beast that makes it a problem, not our desire to have a reasonable amount of material things to make our lives move more smoothly. How much is enough is a never-ending discussion, but there is nothing essentially more spiritual about being poor than being middle class or wealthy. It depends in part on how attached we are to our possessions. (The question of using up more than our share of the planet's resources is, of course, a critical issue for our time that we also need to consider.) In reality, the wanting of material things is often more easily tamed than is our desire for intangibles. The wanting beast is far more insidious in the emotional and psychological realms than in the material. It is about never being satisfied and does not refer to acquiring anything specific. Let's take a look at how the wanting beast shows up in our lives before discussing what we might do about it.

Material Wanting

Have you noticed that sometimes after buying something you have wanted for a long time, you tend not to remain satisfied for very long? We don't want to admit this, because it makes us feel shallow and materialistic, and we think that our family and friends will think less of us if they knew about our inner lust for more. Yet this is a very common human experience. Wanting is habitual and easily becomes obsessive. It is an internal beast that we discover and rediscover the more self-aware we become.

One person might have a two-year-old stereo system and become dissatisfied because he doesn't have the most recent advances, so he goes out and incurs more credit-card debt so he can upgrade. Another person is fixated on another item. Specifics may vary, but most modern people become, to some degree, habitually dependent on buying, acquiring, or in some way possessing things. After attaining these things, we do not necessarily feel the satisfaction we anticipated, but rather after little or no time we develop a new obsession—and so it continues.

From a psychological perspective, there are reasons for this phenomenon, ranging from insecurities carried over from childhood to brain-washing by the media. We could discuss the reasons for our being possessed by the wanting beast and perhaps make our findings the center of a new psychological theory. We might then realize that the entire project had been a product of an obsessive need to gain approval through academic theory building. This kind of circular thinking keeps us locked into old patterns. If we wish to grow, we do not have the luxury of sitting back and accepting the products of our psychological wounding, but rather we need to find creative ways to slip past our obsessions.

Emotional/Psychological Wanting

All of us know people who are seemingly addicted to praise or need more and more proof of others' love for them. Other people crave security to the point that they cannot take a risk, while some fear anything novel or unusual and constantly fight to preserve sameness. Whatever we begin to crave in emotional or psychological realms may engage the wanting beast in the process of getting more and more. We may be fairly certain that the wanting beast is engaged when a person appears to be unable to get enough, whether it be praise, love, security, or stability. It is not that any of these is bad in its own right, as these are reasonable things for humans to want. What is of concern is when they become obsessions and make our lives habitual and driven.

Learning mastery over our psychological and emotional wants is difficult, but that mastery can be attained. First, we need to become aware of our tendencies to overindulge our habitual wanting. The next step is to choose to inhibit our typical responses. Inhibition of emotional desire has gotten a bad reputation in our modern culture; however, when used purposefully and with awareness, it can be an incredible tool for personal growth. Chapter 10, "Developing Mastery," will explain this process more fully.

Spiritual Wanting

We have known for a long time that the spiritual wanting beast is one of the most insidious barriers to spiritual development. This wanting beast takes many forms, but there are two primary forms that we will mention. The first is what we might term "overreaching." The second is often called "spiritual materialism."

A common mistake made by those who are seeking spiritual development is to want the signs of spiritual maturity much sooner than they naturally appear. "Don't push the river" is a saying that all of us who seek spiritual realization would be wise to heed. It takes time to undo years of cultural conditioning and then even more time to heal and revitalize the many layers of our beings. Patience is an absolute necessity for those who tread a spiritual path. Early in your development, you may tend to be much more impatient and perhaps even want marvelous experiences and recognition of your "highness" right away. The truth is that you will need quite a bit of time to strengthen your consciousness and build self-discipline in preparation for the potentially ego-shattering realizations of a spiritual journey.

The second common form taken by the spiritual wanting beast is that of spiritual materialism. This may take many forms, but it is primarily seen in the collection of affirmations of our spiritual development. Some people may aspire to collect initiations in various orders and systems. Initiation may be an exquisite entrance into a path of lifelong growth and development and should not be seen as a reflection of spiritual materialism, but some seek initiation into every new system they encounter and do very little to immerse themselves in the work of the path.

Probably the most insidious form of spiritual materialism may happen to those who take on the role of spiritual guide. Whether this be as priest, pastor, rabbi, mulla, guru, or any other title, the risk is the same. The tendency to believe that this role makes us special is the breeding ground of a narcissistic lifestyle. To be a narcissist is to crave recognition of one's "specialness," and there is very little that makes one more "special" than to have others believe that you have a privileged relationship with the Divine. A sense of humor, humility, and a deep understanding of one's own shadow are essential for those who become spiritual guides. Don't get me wrong—we need people who can teach us about spiritual development, but they have an awesome task in avoiding the spiritual wanting beast of craving admiration and "specialness."

Wishing to transcend, wishing to create, and hundreds of other desires are truly the inner Divine seeking expression. We may embrace much that we desire as part of the God within wishing to manifest. Only when desire becomes obsessive, as seen in the various forms of the wanting beast, are we talking about the subversion of positive qualities. Whether because of a culture that stresses surface accomplishment as opposed to inner accomplishment or because of some innate human desire for recognition or dominance, the wanting beast is a constant companion in most of our lives. When we seek spiritual development, we must learn to deal with this aspect of our shadow.

EXERCISE: *SATTIPATANA*

Sattipatana is a Buddhist practice that systematically disentangles you from your normal identification with body, mind, emotions, personality, and even consciousness itself. It is a particularly useful practice because it helps to neutralize your desires by getting beyond not only the desire itself, but also the part of you that has that desire. For our purposes, although this is not necessarily the case with Buddhism, the task is to avoid being trapped by identification with lower levels of being. This is our version of the practice; it is somewhat different from a traditional version of *sattipatana*. This is a way for you to learn to be in the world without being captured by it. Let's begin the process of exploring and then letting go of your identification with the limited self:

- Get comfortable and go into a meditative state. Follow your breath for a while, concentrating on refining your breathing and clearing your consciousness. Take time to consider deeply the process below, step by step.

- First, consider your body. Of what is it made? How does it work? What is its purpose? Just observe your body as if it were not you. It is made of the same substance as grass, trees, dirt, and animals. Is this you? It functions in ways that are intricate and beautiful, like an amazing machine. Is this you? You have a special relationship with this body. You use it to exist on this planet, but is it who you are, in essence? Who is it, then, who controls your body, disciplines your body when it wants to take over and eat, drink, or smoke more than is healthy. Yes, there is a part of you that uses, controls, and appreciates this piece of flesh and bone that you normally identify with. Who is that?

- Your mind seems to have some control over your body; is that who you are—your mind? You spend most of your life thinking, planning, hoping, remembering, and anticipating; is this who you are in your essence, your apparatus for thinking—your mind? Your mind is an incredible creation, almost beyond comprehension, but is it not *your* mind? Who is the "you" that your mind serves? Who is it who must bring your mind into balance when it becomes cloudy, fixated, foolish, or wandering? Who must be the master of your mind? If you are not simply your body or your mind, then who are you?

- You might think that maybe you *are* your emotions. Certainly, emotions often feel more primary than thoughts. Your emotions are often a better gauge of what is going on than your mind, which is so easily deluded. Does this mean that the true and essential you is to be found in your emotions? Certainly, emotions like love can be transcendent, but emotions are usually reactive and dependent on external stimuli. You feel in reaction to something outside of yourself. Can something that is a reaction be the essential you? Who is it who is reacting? Whoever that is must come before the reaction, so your emotions can't be the essential you.

- Your personality, which is a combination of all that we have been discussing as well as inherited traits, both physical and spiritual, is certainly a much broader concept of self. Are you essentially your personality? Is that as deep as it goes? Your personality is an accumulation of characteristics and qualities focused around the seed of you. You sometimes find aspects of your personality that you want to change and then do so. Who is it who wants to change and then effects that change? It must be that seed around which the personality has grown that is the true you. What is this deep part of yourself that holds all aspects of your being and is what you mean when you say "I"?

• Consciousness is essential to being. The term *soul* could be used interchangeably with consciousness to define who we often feel is our essential self. Consciousness/soul is that seed of self that accumulates all that becomes "you" over time. Is this who you are at the deepest, most essential level? Possibly, but consciousness is still dependent. Consciousness involves duality. There is always the consciousness and that of which it is conscious. If you are truly a part of the One, then there must be a non-dual you that is beyond consciousness. Consciousness is the externalization of intelligence, or what mystics call Spirit.

• Can you briefly step beyond even consciousness and become pure intelligence, pure spirit? Let go briefly of all your identifications with things that are transient, even soul. Enter the world of your essential nature, your essential self, the world of pure intelligence and capacity, prior to creation. This can be your baseline of who you are. Pure spirit.

- You are alive for a purpose, not simply to remain in a state of pure, undifferentiated intelligence. Therefore, you do not go to this high place to escape your life, but rather to make it more beautiful. When you experience *sattipatana*, it becomes easier to let go of the wanting beast and follow the bliss that is your life's purpose.

In the chapter that follows, "Intending a Spiritual Life," we will discuss ways to move beyond our wants and into the realm of the will, and we will explore ways to use our *intention* to propel us further on our spiritual journeys.

eight

Intending a Spiritual Life

Intention is at the core of all spiritual development. The fact that you are reading this book means that at a conscious level, you probably have some degree of intention related to developing spiritually. You may have already noticed that intention works at both conscious and unconscious levels; it is quite possible to live large portions of our lives without a conscious understanding of our true intentions.

Moments of choice and free will arrive because we intend, from a very deep place, either consciously or unconsciously, to change and grow. Moments of choice may become opportunities to align your life with your intentions. In the case of life-changing choices, you will often face a struggle; deciding to make the changes necessary to follow your heart's desire is not easy. You may face several instances of choice before you figure out what is happening and are able follow your inner intention into a new phase of life. You may find that when you take the first steps in a new direction, you encounter obstacles, as you have not yet created new "grooves" for your life to follow. You might compare your old, habitual ways of living to a train that is following an established set of tracks; if you want to go somewhere else, it will take time and persistence to lay a new set of tracks and begin to follow them.

Nevertheless, once put in motion by choice and followed with persistence, changes will set you upon a course that will lead toward your desired goal. Often, you will be amazed by coincidence, happenstance, serendipity, luck, blessings, and grace as your new path unfolds before you, but the key feature that begins all of this is your intention. This is a secret of life: this path will continue to unfold until some other choice, based on deep intention, intervenes to change your life's direction. Far too often we may believe that we have no choice about how our lives are unfolding, and it is true that life is unpredictable, but when we become aware of our intentions and take responsibility for our choices, the truth of our lives' paths becomes visible.

There are a couple of keys to working with intention: awareness and will. Awareness has to do with becoming conscious of the intention that has been operating in your life as well as becoming conscious of a new or deeper intention that wants to emerge. Will is the power that resides within and can align with your deeper intention and change your direction. Let's take a closer look at these two capabilities.

Awareness

Awareness involves becoming conscious—making known what had been ignored or unknown. In the area of intention, you need to become aware of what you desire, as well as your current condition. Often, you begin this process by seeing what you desire for yourself in another. For example, you might see a quality or condition in another and wish that you were like that person. This is a lifelong process that begins when you are a small child and admire and identify with your parent (or a surrogate) for being so big and capable. You continue to admire and identify with friends, teachers, and mentors as you grow and mature. They become your role models, and you hope to become like them someday, a process that is a primary way of learning our roles in society. The interesting part of this process is that you identify with role models based on affinity. You can best identify with those who display attributes that are latent within your own being. People with spiritual tendencies often become aware of their own deep natures by witnessing the signs of spiritual development in others. You may admire and seek to find out how these individuals have come to manifest the qualities you desire. In a process of the externalization of the inner intention to manifest your own spiritual nature, you may choose to seek guidance from someone whom you admire. There is little difference between these dynamics and those of a five-year-old girl who wants to be like her mother; by emulating her mother, she learns, if all goes well, how to grow into a capable woman. Exemplars are needed at all stages of human development and need to be honored; however, it is the intention within that draws you toward the example. The same intention will draw you away when it is time to stop externalizing and to start incorporating into your being the qualities that your role model symbolizes for you.

While you have been admiring others over a period of time, you may have begun to make your own nature more conscious, which will lead to the recognition that what you have been seeking is indeed a part of yourself. You may have become painfully aware of the ways in which you have not yet become what you intend to be. This is another inevitable aspect of becoming aware; you realize the degree to which you are not living up to your ideals.

Trying to become like your role models is not the only way in which you become aware of your desires and latent potentialities. Your awareness may grow through experiences that trigger new realizations. Dreams, visions, and "aha!" experiences may bring new direction to your life. The normal process of growth and maturity may catapult you into directions that you may have never considered during another stage of your life. You may also notice that your life is becoming humdrum or boring or lacking apparent purpose. Even people who are fulfilling previous dreams may find that, upon completion, those dreams were too small, and their realization feels surprisingly empty.

Change, or the perceived need for change, may cause a crisis in your life. People may change consciously and joyfully, or people may change through pain—many of us unconsciously choose pain. Change usually percolates upward for a long time before finally becoming conscious. During this process, you may feel disillusionment with your life, emptiness, lethargy, depression, or, for people on a spiritual path, a crisis of faith. As we discussed previously, what St. John of the Cross called "the dark night of the soul" often precedes major spiritual breakthroughs. This happens in part because you are unaware of the unconscious changes in intention that are percolating upward from the depths of your being; those unconscious shifts in intention may render your old way of life somewhat meaningless, regardless of what your head says. We in Western societies, because of our mind-oriented culture, expect that we will always be aware of the really important things going on in our psyches. The truth is that much of what is truly important in our lives happens beneath the surface, and we may know very little about ourselves for a long time. Intention is always working behind the scenes.

Will

Will involves the capacity to exert direction and control over your life. It involves choosing and carrying out your choices. Mystics, philosophers, and people of faith tend to divide will into personal will versus "God's will," "the higher will," "divine will," and other such labels. These are often useful distinctions, but they do imply an exaggerated sense of otherness between the human and the transcendent. As one grows spiritually, that distinction is, to varying degrees, reconciled. The central question is, "Who is it who is willing?" In an earlier chapter, we clarified that for us, "higher will" is the function of a living, awakened heart—a heart that has broken out of the confines of an ego-bound world and is attuned to the universal. When one is almost completely oblivious to one's deepest intentions, bound instead to the small perspective of the individual ego, the way most of us start out, the dichotomy of "higher" and "lower" is quite valid. As you become aware of your true motivations and begin to choose from that perspective, the separation between upper and lower, sacred and profane, even God and human, begins to fade. At that point, your living heart begins to carry the divine intention; your heart's desire becomes aligned with—almost inseparable from—what some might call "God's will" or the pattern of the universe. For this to happen, you must stay aware of and remain true to your heart's intention— and its relationship to the unity of life. Awareness again is the key.

You may be concerned about having too much willfulness, and it's true that willfulness may be a sign of both an undeveloped will and being out of touch with your true nature. When you are tuned in to the intention of your soul, your awakened heart, will is not willful—it flows. There are times when things flow exactly as they need to in order for you to accomplish your heart's desire; it is at these times that your true will can be seen in action.

EXERCISE: DISCOVERING YOUR DEEP INTENTIONS

This exercise is designed to guide you through an exploration of your intentions, systematically leading you inward toward your deepest intentions, which are often unconscious.

- Begin by exploring what you believe are your main intentions for your life right now. They may be things like finding a good or better job, finding someone to love, or moving somewhere to find a better life.

- These intentions may seem reasonable, but do they come from your heart? Are they intentions that are essential enough to guide every aspect of your life? If not, then go deeper. Find the intention behind the various intentions that you are working with every day. What do your desires have in common? What are you searching for that is bigger or more essential than the specific intentions that you have already uncovered?

- Discover underlying themes in your surface intentions. They may be themes such as "I desire the power to make things better for the people I care about (or the world)" or "My life is dedicated to loving service" or "I will earn the respect of others." Look deeply and find the underlying theme for all of your intentions.

- Now find the essence that motivates your life. Is it love? Is it service? Is it healing? Is it mastery? Is it enlightenment? Everyone has a core intention that is acting behind all other motivations. What is yours?

- When you discover a core intention, you will have found the essence of your being and will possess a key that can unlock many secrets in your life. If you have not yet found this core intention or are unsure about it, then be assured that you have asked the most important question of your life and are set upon a path that will lead you to the truth of your own being. Don't be discouraged; it takes many years for most of us to unlock this secret.

The next chapter, "Creating a Living Heart," will help you to energize and work with the powerful heart center, the place where the most important of all spiritual development takes place.

nine

Creating a Living Heart

When most of us consider spiritual development, we think about developing our minds or connecting with spiritual realms. Seldom do we realize that it is through the feeling nature—our hearts—that most of the real spiritual work is done. It is primarily through an awakened and living heart that spiritual realms are reached. Our minds are but the surface of the deep well of being that is our hearts. Spiritual development begins and ends with awakening, purifying, strengthening, refining, and expanding our heart qualities. Consciousness itself develops through awakening, purifying, strengthening, refining, and expanding the deep feeling nature. When consciousness is fed only through the mind, it remains narrow and undernourished, but when it also receives sustenance from the heart, it can take its rightful place in life. The will is involved also; the will intends, and the living heart embodies. A living heart is the crucible in which all things intended by the awakened will are forged, and it is also the accommodation for the deep wisdom revealed through spiritual development.

Obviously, we are not talking about the physical pump contained within our chests. We are referring to qualities that are related to the emotional life, qualities that belong to the energy center called the heart chakra. We discussed energy centers, or chakras, in chapter 4, "The Spiritual Architecture of the Self." To refresh your memory, the word *chakra* literally means "wheel" and refers to swirling vortexes in the human aura that serve as centers for certain types of energy.

There is a qualitative difference between heart emotions and the emotions often associated with energy centers located at the solar plexus, navel, or root chakras. Heart emotions are generally related to love, compassion, care, and joy. They may also include strength and courage, especially in service of others. Emotions associated with power and dominance tend to be related to the solar plexus, and passions of many sorts relate to the navel chakra. Emotions concerned with basic needs and survival belong to the root chakra.

When talking about creating a living heart as an aspect of spiritual development, we are referring to working with the emotions of the heart chakra. These emotions unite where there is division and heal where there is wounding. They pull the world together to seek connections, rather than dividing the world through judging and evaluating. Emotions such as love, kindness, compassion, and empathy fill the lonely void of our separate existence with the joy of interconnectedness. One difference between the spiritually realized person and others is the degree of interconnectedness experienced by the former. As the rigid separateness between self and all else becomes moderated through spiritual practice, those who are spiritually awake with living hearts begin to know the experience of others, human or otherwise. When a heart that is alive crosses boundaries, veils are lifted, and the heart is able to see all things.

Bringing your heart to life is a process that takes time, as well it should, for without sufficient preparation, these changes could be catastrophic to the limited ego. Some persons with fragile ego boundaries may experience in daily life small amounts of merging. Because they lack the knowledge and strength required to maintain their own personal boundaries, they may become overwhelmed by others, as well as by emotional upheaval. Psychological problems ranging from anxiety disorders and depression to schizophrenia may be related in part to the lack of sufficient boundaries between self and other. The task is to develop sufficiently strong ego boundaries early in life to avoid being overwhelmed by the world; with this solid foundation, one may then begin to expand the heart through love and compassion.

Opening the Heart

What we are calling "creating a living heart" has sometimes been referred to as "opening the heart." There are ways, in addition to expanding the feeling nature, to develop spiritually, but all paths must address the heart in time, because it is only through a living heart that spiritual adulthood can be reached. Paths that work primarily with the mind must eventually moderate the mind's realizations with love, or else the sage becomes the cynic. Paths that stress service, such as karma yoga, often rely on developing heart qualities to motivate one's work. Paths of the heart may stand alone for a while, but eventually, increasing knowledge and the desire to serve others emerge as natural consequences. Opening and awakening the heart are essential at some point along the path, so let's explore the workings of this process.

The vast majority of us in Western societies have hearts that are wounded. We emerge from childhood with scars from too little parenting, too much indulgence, too many instances of feeling like failures, and too often having to suppress our own feelings and needs to fit into the institutions of society. Some of us were physically or emotionally abused while growing up by those who should have protected us, and many of us cut off parts of our selves in order to survive in school systems. The list of sources of wounding is endless, yet it is this very wounding that motivates us to grow. If it were not for our wounds, we might be content to live our lives without questioning, and it is in the questioning that we discover that there is more to life than meets the eye.

Wounding, however, often makes us overly protective of our hearts. When we guard our hearts, they are not open to others and to new experiences. Feeling wounded, we crawl within the safety of habits and sameness and avoid that which is different or strange to us. Wounds often motivate us to distrust others, to avoid the possibility of being wounded again. Some people's wounds have made them more vulnerable by convincing them that they are not entitled to have boundaries or to say no to demands placed on them. Just as there are countless potential causes for wounds, there are also countless ways to respond to the wounds. The first step in healing the heart is to accept our woundedness and take some steps toward building awareness of the patterns in our lives that are related to the wounds. It is not necessary to solve all of our problems to do spiritual work—if that were the case, none of us would ever get to it. What is more likely is that our psychological work and spiritual work together will develop a synergy in which growth in one area opens up new vistas in the other.

Each of us is a whole, multidimensional being with physical, emotional, mental, and spiritual facets. The rewarding work of bringing your heart to life is done within the context of the rest of your life. Most of us are not allowed the luxury afforded to the hermits and monks of previous generations, who could sometimes methodically isolate themselves from their environments and work on specific tasks without interference from life's little surprises (although that was seldom totally achieved). Today, we have the privilege and challenge of doing our spiritual work in the middle of our daily lives. Amidst family, friends, coworkers, and bosses, we are called to find our hearts and live our highest ideals. A few years ago, Richard and a friend, a practitioner of Zen Buddhism, had a long discussion about whether it was possible to reach enlightenment while living a daily life of work and family. We are now convinced that it is possible and that this is the way of the future.

Today, you may use everyday life to perfect your heart. You may concentrate on loving your spouse, friends, children, and parents—including their flaws and despite the hurts that they cause you. You may attempt to remain emotionally and intellectually courageous amidst work situations that make you feel small and powerless. You may take care that whenever you use power in your life, you proceed with the desire to serve others—without infringing on their ability to determine the courses of their own lives. You may keep your heart open in situations that would normally cause you to feel anger and rejection. None of these possibilities is easy, yet all of them provide incredible opportunities to master your less-refined instincts and to affirm the emotions of the heart.

Because of the difficulty in accomplishing such tasks, you may need practices to help you to prepare for living your spirituality in everyday life. In order to strengthen your ability to remain centered in your heart amidst the challenges of daily life, we will suggest some practices that you might use. Some of these have ancient roots, and others have emerged more recently. We will outline three types of practices that will build the capacity to live life from a kind, loving, and emotionally courageous place, the living heart.

Seeing Beauty

The first practice is to endeavor to see beauty. Whenever possible, take the time to notice the beauty around you. Some things are obviously beautiful—flowers, sunsets, your lover's smile, and your children's moments of delight. Take the time to notice these obvious, beautiful things in your life as often as you possibly can. Instead of walking quickly past the rose blooming in your front yard as you leave for work, pause and smell the rose, and enjoy its transient loveliness for a moment. When your child comes to you in wide-eyed wonder to tell you about the butterfly she just saw, enter that world of wonder with her and allow yourself to be transfixed by her eyes.

Taking time to notice the beauty of the world we inhabit is one of the great gifts of life, and one that can be transforming. Chapter 13, "Connecting with Nature," includes several more examples of ways to work with beauty in the natural world.

Using Sound

The heart chakra, just like all other centers, may be influenced by the use of sound. Sound is useful in purifying and preparing the heart for deeper spiritual work. As we noted in chapter 5, "Spiritual Practices," the vibration created by the sound "aah" is what does the work. If we think about the names given to the One Being in many cultures, we can see the centrality of the "aah" sound. *Brahma*, from the Hindu tradition; *Allah*, from the Muslim tradition; and even the English word *God* all contain the soft, rich "aah" sound. Most cultures have traditions that involve singing or chanting in order to alter consciousness. Any songs, chants, *wasaif,* or mantras that use the "aah" sound are useful in purifying, tuning, and strengthening the heart.

To review from chapter 5, using sound is a shortcut in the long and sometimes arduous process of spiritual development. Sound practices are used in many schools of inner study, because they exert a powerful vibratory influence over our subtle bodies and can act to increase our receptivity to spiritual growth. To get a feel for the way sound practices work on the heart center, intone the syllable "saah" for two minutes. Keep the sound going, pausing only to take breaths. You will notice that this sound resonates in your heart center and makes the center feel stronger and more alive.

Refining Emotions

Eventually, after opening your heart to beauty, love, empathy, and wonder, you will become ready to take on the task of watching, controlling, and refining your emotions. Through the processes mentioned above, many of your least favorite emotions will fall away, because you will become less attached to them. As you become awestruck by the beauty in life, you have less room for hatred. As you develop compassion for others, the self-pity you once felt no longer holds the same grip on you. As you love deeply, your existential loneliness fades. Some old, ingrained emotional habits may still persist, so the advanced spiritual adept eventually needs to begin to deal with them before moving on. The further you proceed with your spiritual development, the more you will find the need to master your emotions; as you develop wisdom and magnetism, your unresolved emotional issues carry more clout and may do harm to yourself and others. The history of a few spiritual leaders who have led their followers down disastrous paths is there for all to see. All of us are human and we all have our issues, but the sage must take more responsibility than the average person for keeping his or her unresolved emotional issues in check.

Heart Meditation

This is our favorite heart meditation. It uses your breath, the golden heart color, and expansive visualization to create an experience of the vastness and true nature of your heart. Take your time and enjoy!

- As you inhale, locate a small golden orb in the center of your chest in the region of your physical heart, and notice that your attention causes it to glow brighter. As you exhale, notice that the golden orb begins to expand.

- As you inhale again, notice that the orb grows brighter still, and as you exhale, see that it expands even more. Get used to this rhythm, because soon it is going to propel you beyond the physical boundaries that normally restrict you.

- Each time you inhale, you experience the orb becoming brighter, and each time you exhale, it expands to encompass a larger aspect of your reality. Keep using your breath as a mechanism to focus your concentration as you expand to encompass:

  - Your chest
  - Your body
  - A large sphere around your body
  - The room
  - Your home
  - Your neighborhood
  - Your town or city
  - Your state
  - Your region
  - Your nation
  - Your hemisphere
  - The world
  - The earth and moon
  - The solar system
  - The Milky Way galaxy
  - The entire cosmos
  - The nonphysical universe, along with the physical universe

- Now allow yourself to feel this expanded nature of self. Everything, "everywhere and always," exists within your heart. Let the feeling last and expand if it wishes. Know that this is your true nature.

- When you reach a point at which you feel finished with the concentration, slowly return to everyday awareness, but keep the memory of your vastness fresh and make sure that the golden orb is glowing bright within and around your body. (If you find that you don't wish to return, take a deep inhalation to bring yourself back.)

- You may return to your visualization of the golden orb at any time, and it will remind you of the vastness of your living heart, which is your true inheritance.

Once you have begun to awaken your heart, you will find that one of the next steps in spiritual development is to increase your capacity to master your emotions as well as the circumstances of your life. This process, addressed in the next chapter, "Developing Mastery," will help you to channel your energy productively and will increase your magnetism.

ten

Developing Mastery

To become the person who you wish to be, you will need to become the doer at the center of all your actions. Gradually, you will learn to develop sufficient self-discipline so that your actions come from your inner being and not from impulse or habit. This is not because of a "should" imposed by an authority figure, but rather because mastery is needed at every stage of spiritual development, to facilitate awakening as well as to continue growing after awakening. Mastery, the self-possession that puts the essential you in charge of yourself, may be the most important prerequisite for awakening. When you move past habitual ways of relating to existence, as well as blind, impulsive actions, and begin to live each moment from your heart, you will have gained a degree of mastery and awakening. Even those who may seem to be totally awake or enlightened must be vigilant constantly to maintain their mastery. Awakened beings have greater power and responsibility and can make far more disastrous mistakes if they lose focus.

Mastery may be developed in all domains of life. You can develop mastery over your body, mind, and emotions, and in doing so, your true self begins to take over as the primary actor in your life. Much of what you will do in the process of spiritual development is designed to improve your self-discipline and mindfulness, which are at the heart of developing mastery. There is more to mastery than self-discipline and mindfulness, however; the seeds of self-mastery eventually develop into mastery over your environment and, ultimately, over life. Mastery may be seen as the vehicle for your awakened heart. The self-discipline, mindfulness, and power that evolve into mastery serve to channel the willfulness of the lower self into something productive. Beyond that, they become the power behind the awakened will of your heart. Like everything else in spiritual development, mastery takes time and is best approached as a process to be played out systematically over the course of your development. Moving too zealously might be overly stressful for most people, so we recommend a gentle but firm middle way as the most reasonable approach.

Most traditions have had practices designed to promote mastery in the lives of their adherents, but over time the original purposes of these practices often have become lost. The Christian practice of Lent is a good example. If you ask many Christians why they give something up for Lent, they may explain that this is a period of preparation for the blessings of Easter. In addition to this, Lent has a far deeper significance. The austerities prescribed for Lent are an exercise in mastery to prepare our inner beings to receive that which they would not normally be able to assimilate. Early Christians still retained some understanding of the nature of spiritual progress and knew that the self-discipline developed by doing some partial fasting and engaging in forty days of Lenten rituals would help to prepare for the Christian miracle of Easter.

Similarly, the Buddha spent several years practicing severe austerities, preparing himself to attain enlightenment, and even when it came time to attain Buddhahood, he still, according to tradition, had to spend forty-nine days and nights sitting under the Bodhi tree. He followed a long line of practitioners of the yoga of the day; they recognized the power of attaining mastery through self-discipline.

The depth of understanding of the traditions of renunciation and self-discipline has been lost to most groups. It is important to realize, as did the Buddha, that austerity may become an ego trip and sometimes may do more harm than good. We live in times that are quite different from the days when some tried to develop mastery by putting knitting needles through their noses or by standing on one leg for weeks, techniques that are no longer appropriate for spiritual development. Extreme austerities provide little help in getting past our egos. It may now be more appropriate to use mastery to refrain from showing our abilities to rise above our environment rather than to stand out in a crowd. Mastery over your habitual physical, mental, and emotional patterns will allow your true self the opportunity to be the primary mover in your life. Let's look at each of these domains a little more closely.

Physical Mastery

As we begin to explore the domain of physical mastery, you might ask yourself a few questions: "Do I see my body as something over which I have very little control?" "Am I sometimes a slave to my cravings?" "Do I have physical habits that are detrimental to my physical and psychological well-being?" If you answered yes to one or more of the above, congratulations—you're "normal." But "normal" is not what we are seeking in spiritual development; we're seeking mastery. Being normal gives you an opportunity! In other words, you have some of the above issues to work on. You may begin to look for cravings and habits that can be mastered. Don't try to give something up because someone is telling you to do so, but rather because you recognize that your body cannot serve two masters. Either your craving is in charge of you, or *you* are in charge of you. You might ask yourself which it will be. This attitude may transform complaining about a diet or about having to quit smoking into a sense of accomplishment and control. Once you have the self-discipline to refrain from habitual activities at will, then you may add the component of not bragging about it. If you are able not only to abstain from the activity but also to avoid the satisfaction of telling others about your self-discipline, you will have made a powerful step toward authentic selfhood.

Mental Mastery

We will divide mental mastery into two categories: impulse control and control over your thoughts. Impulse control is closely aligned with the physical control of cravings and habits but may be most successfully dealt with at the mental level. Impulses are automatic responses to environmental stimuli. Whenever you automatically react, you are in the realm of habit and impulse. Sometimes this is appropriate, as in the case of ducking when you are about to hit your head, but at other times an impulse, such as wanting to yell at someone who cuts you off in traffic, may not be appropriate.

Mastery of your impulses involves becoming aware of the thoughts that precede the impulse and inhibiting the physical response. For instance, in the case of being cut off in traffic, you might first notice your response to the incident (quickened pulse and rising anger), then notice the thoughts that are going through your mind ("What an idiot!"), and then intervene with a response that feels as if it is coming from your spiritual self and not your habitual self. Possibly your response in this instance would be to chuckle to yourself, saying something like, "Maybe they had a hard day." The important thing is that the response be chosen, not automatic. Impulse control is a powerful means of developing mastery, as long as it is not done as a "should" imposed by an external authority, but rather as a desire of your higher self.

Controlling your thoughts is a much more difficult process and may be overwhelming if you have not built up strength through physical self-discipline and impulse control. Do you have habitual thoughts that keep you from fully living your life? Do you hear yourself saying, "Oh, I couldn't do that" or "I'm not capable" or "I'm too lazy"? There are countless ways in which we talk to ourselves that are not very useful; they deny our true potential. Here are a few more questions to ask yourself: Do I seem to think in only one direction? Am I always right? Always wrong? Do I always have to win? Always have to lose? These sorts of life scripts are aspects of mental patterns that constrain our options in life. If we are to escape living our lives as automatons and become authentic human beings, we need to observe these patterns and gradually transform them into more helpful ways of thinking.

To change these patterns of thought, you first need to become aware of them and then assert your will to change them. The first step is to begin to watch your thoughts. You will find that developing and paying attention to that reflective aspect of yourself that watches is a great help. The next step is to separate yourself enough from your thoughts that you can evaluate them as habits. For instance, is it reasonable that you should always respond to others by thinking they are right and you are wrong? When you begin to realize that your thoughts are habitual and not reasonable responses to your life, you may start to generate alternative ways of thinking. Finally, you may begin to substitute more authentic thoughts for those that you now recognize as habitual patterns that are products of past experiences but unrelated to the realities of who you are becoming.

Emotional Mastery

For some people, the emotions, more than our bodies and minds, may seem somewhat inaccessible and maybe even mysterious. For others, the emotions often seem more essentially *you* than anything else; there is a reason for that— they *are*. You may find that you can fool yourself with your thoughts and words, but your emotions often tell you what is real. One very good means of building intuition is to check how a possible action makes you feel when you are evaluating it. It is especially helpful to become aware of how ideas or events affect your heart center, the seat of "higher" emotions.

How might we learn to channel or discipline our emotions? We might ask ourselves more questions: "Am I sometimes moody?" "Do I have trouble controlling my temper?" "Am I always falling in love with the wrong person?" "Are my head and heart often in conflict?" If any of the above questions caught your attention, you know that emotions can be a double-edged sword. Emotions may reveal, and emotions may obscure. Your emotions may help you follow your true heart's desire in life, and your emotions may make your life unbearable. Some emotions are old, stale patterns that have built up over time as responses to your world. Other emotions are fresh experiences derived from what you are encountering in the moment. The trick is learning to discern the difference.

As with mental patterns, emotional mastery begins with awareness. You first learn to watch your emotions as they ebb and flow. You notice the patterns and pay attention to what feels real and authentic in the moment and what feels as though it is habitual and only partially related to your life at the moment. Awareness can be transformative, and even before you make any conscious effort to change your emotions, they may begin to change on their own. If you have a particularly difficult emotional habit—and most of us do—the next step may be one of the hardest things you will ever do. Inhibiting emotional patterns such as moodiness or resentment will take constant awareness, but it will also take—even more importantly—a great deal of emotional strength, built through the practice of physical and mental mastery. Emotional mastery should not be undertaken until you feel strong as a result of considerable prior success in self-discipline and mindfulness; overstressing yourself serves no purpose. When you are ready, the payoff for this kind of mastery is great, because what develops is a sense that you are a spiritual person who is capable of following the intention of your soul.

Exercise: Gaining Mastery

Giving up things is one of the most effective techniques for developing mastery. Recognizing that ongoing daily mastery over things like temper, self-destructive habits, and fear of change is the work of the mastery that you build, it is important occasionally to impose mastery-building restrictions upon yourself. This may be done in many arenas of life, but it is advisable to begin with physical mastery, since it is the easiest. Once you have had some success with giving up something physical, you may take the next step of giving up something in a mental or emotional arena.

When you choose to give up something, please note the following suggestions:

- What you give up should be something that you like or value.

- At first, what you give up should not be something that will require extreme sacrifice that you are not likely to be able to accomplish. Your first few attempts at building this sort of mastery should consider your likelihood of success.

- Remember that this is an exercise in self-discipline and not a condemnation of what it is that you are giving up. You may give anything up, including fruits and vegetables, as long as it is something that you really desire—but we do not suggest giving up anything that is important to your health. (Let's imagine for the moment that you decide to give up chocolate.)

Think about how long you are willing to give up what you have chosen. Pick a reasonable length of time. We suggest a week or ten days at the beginning. Not only will that keep this exercise fresh, but it will also give you the opportunity to pick something else, maybe something more difficult, when you have succeeded and while you are still committed to the process.

Now add these thoughts to this process:

- Each time you are tempted to eat chocolate (or whatever you have chosen to give up), in addition to inhibiting the impulse, remember that by doing so you are making sure that it is you that is charge of your choices in life, and not chocolate.

- Instead of telling others about what you are doing, tell yourself that by remaining quiet about your successes, you are conserving the power that you are building for use in becoming more masterful.

After you have had success with physical self-discipline, you may work for a while on emotional impulse control. For instance, you could inhibit your impulses to react angrily to other drivers while driving, or you could resist the temptation to succumb to peer pressure to go drinking after work. It is good to do a big giving-up every once in a while, just to build mastery and to remember who is in charge of your life. There are some people, however, who may become addicted to giving up. If you are one who is able to get into the habit of giving things up easily and you find yourself becoming a compulsive renunciate, you will need to give up giving up! Mastery is about getting beyond habitual patterns, and if you find yourself engaging in habitual giving up, you will need to go back to the drawing board and find other ways to develop mastery. Again, the classical "middle way" is the most reasonable choice.

The next chapter is devoted to learning how to meditate, a topic that will probably be somewhat less demanding than that of developing mastery!

eleven

Meditation

Meditation is a broad term used to refer to a nearly endless number of ways that have been used for millennia to train the mind and focus it on spiritual themes. As you learn to meditate, you will develop the skills of concentrating, focusing on a theme, and using mental imaging. Eliminating unwanted, habitual thoughts is a part of meditation. Although meditation and spiritual development might appear to be synonymous in the popular culture of Western countries, there are differences. Meditation is one or more of many techniques for training and focusing the mind that are used for spiritual development and is an important part of many spiritual paths.

Beginning to Meditate

If you have not yet begun a regular regimen of meditation, you are probably ready to learn how to begin. If you have already started meditating, you may wish to use this information to refine your current practice.

Preparing a space is the first step. It is good to have one place in your environment to which you can retreat; this special place will help to remind you of your intention. You will want this space to be as peaceful and as aesthetically pleasing as you can make it. It should be out of the major traffic flow in your home and as private as possible. Next, you will want to put in this space a few well-chosen objects that remind you of the inner life and the beauty of your heart. Many people create a small altar and arrange meaningful objects there. If the natural world speaks to you, these might be items that represent the four elements or the four directions. If you identify with a particular religion, then you might choose symbolic objects that are sacred to your religion. If the underlying unity of religious ideals or spiritual paths is meaningful to you, you might put objects related to several religions or spiritual paths on the altar. Typically, people also place on the altar a candle to represent the kindling of the inner light or the presence of the divine light, and many burn incense that represents their prayers or meditations rising to the heavens.

What is more important than any of the above is that the objects that you place in this space help you to keep your heart open and remind you of your spiritual quest. If you live in a crowded space with little privacy, you might have just one object in a drawer that you can retrieve and place on a tabletop to create your meditation space, or you might dispense with the idea of objects. Your intention will carry you, regardless.

The next thing you need to think about is your position. The first consideration is to be comfortable so that you can maintain a quiet and still body for a while, but you do not want to be so comfortable that you fall asleep! For this reason, sitting cross-legged on a firm pillow works well for some. If your body is relatively supple, this might be the best choice, but if your body is not quite as flexible as you might like, the best alternative might be a straight-backed chair. Many Westerners who have not grown up sitting cross-legged do better in a chair, although some of us who learned to sit cross-legged like the sense of being grounded that one gets from sitting on the floor or the ground. A few people like to kneel on wooden kneeling benches. What matters is that your position works for you. The second important thing about sitting is that your spine needs to be straight. A straight spine aids the flow of energy and helps in visualizations that deal with energy flow. This is why we suggest a straight-backed chair rather than a lounge chair.

Some people recommend music for meditating; the appropriate music may be helpful in elevating or deepening your consciousness. The topic of choosing music for meditation can be vast. We live in a sea of vibration, and music consists of vibrations attuned to specific planes of being. Because of this, different sorts of music will carry you to different planes, to different levels of consciousness; you may see that choosing the music that will be most helpful for your meditations at each stage in your spiritual unfolding is an art, if not a science. Both knowledge of music and keen intuition will help in making appropriate choices.

You might explore a range of music, from Gregorian chant to Tibetan chanting to Native American flute music—the possibilities are endless. The important consideration is that the music quiets you and has a beneficial effect on your consciousness. You will want to avoid music that is not in resonance with your state, as it might eclipse your meditation process. As you learn to meditate, you can experiment with starting a meditation session by listening to a piece of music that you find helpful. In general, however, we recommend that at first you turn the music off and do most of your meditative practices in silence. To get started with a meditative practice, you will want your own heart, your own energy, and your own intentions to carry you most of the time. Music used as a tune-up during your daily routines is wonderful, and we have experienced carefully chosen music used during spiritual retreats as a magnificent vehicle that carries the consciousness into vast realms.

The final aspect of beginning a meditative practice is picking a regular time to meditate. We suggest that you attempt to meditate at this same time each day. Some people find that getting up twenty minutes earlier in the morning and meditating before the start of the day is best. The advantage to morning meditation is that it tunes you up for the day, and your day will tend to go much better. Some people find that the same time each evening works better for them. Meditating twice a day, even for short periods of time, will tend to accelerate your progress, if you are able to adjust your life to do it. Ultimately, your schedule will depend on your individual preference. The important thing is that you develop a rhythm and meditate at the same time, or times, each day.

All of the above suggestions will help meditation become an integral part of your life and will make it easier to learn to meditate. After you have practiced for a while, you will notice that when you enter your sacred space, you automatically go into a meditative mode. You may also notice that your body and mind begin to expect to meditate when you sit in a particular position or at a certain time of the day. In other words, you will be using classical conditioning techniques to make it easier for you to meditate.

Types of Meditation

In his previous book, *Authentic Spirituality,* Richard divided meditation into concentration, active meditation, and passive meditation; the book also discussed creative imagination. You might wish to refer to it for more detailed explanations of active and passive meditation. Dividing meditation practice into recognizable categories is an attempt to distill the thousands of different meditation techniques that exist in the world. Virtually every religion, indigenous tradition, and spiritual school has developed the means to train the mind and focus the individual practitioner on the spiritual ideal. The various versions of meditative practice are simply the cultural inflections of a universal practice. After looking at these broad categories, we will explore some specific techniques in more detail. We will conclude this chapter with a discussion of creative imagination, as it is central to understanding what the mind encounters in the process of meditation.

Concentration

The more you advance in spiritual practice, the more you will need the tool of a well-developed ability to concentrate. It is for this reason that many beginning meditation techniques require that you develop concentration. The first benefit of concentration is that it will help you to set aside all of the other aspects of your life in order to meditate each day. Once you start meditating, you may find that your body will begin to rebel against sitting still, and you may struggle to complete your practices; through this struggle, you will be developing concentration and mastery. There are some specific techniques that may require you to gaze at an object for long periods of time (looking at a nail in the wall is one classic example) or to contemplate a pattern, such as a Tibetan Buddhist mandala. Most of these techniques have several purposes, but paramount among them is developing your power of concentration.

Not all methods for developing concentration need be meditations, as Richard has discovered:

I found that in my life, the most beneficial practice for developing my ability to concentrate was the approximately fourteen years I spent doing psychotherapy. I discovered that in order to be effective as a therapist, whether with individuals, couples, families, or small groups, I had to be in a state of heightened awareness and attuned to every cue the client gave me. I got to the point that I became so aware of the client that I had little awareness of self, the ideal state in meditation. It was only the natural rhythm of the world of therapy that compelled me to notice the time at the end of a counseling session. It is this same kind of absorption that marks the successful development of concentration.

You may have noticed that normally your mind is only partially under your control. Much that goes on in your thinking process is what we call "roof-brain chatter," or random thoughts, and only some of it makes you feel good. When your mind is full of unwanted clutter—some call it the "monkey mind"—there is little room for peace, joy, or ecstasy. Concentration serves the purpose of mental purification, and as you improve your concentration over time, you will notice that your habitual patterns of thinking will change as well. Your mind will be quieter, less filled with unwanted, habitual thoughts, and more capable of both receptivity and creativity.

Exercise: A Concentration Practice

Take out a blank sheet of white 8½ × 11 inch paper, a compass (the type used to draw a circle), and a black felt-tipped pen. Using the compass and your felt-tipped pen, create a circle of the size that will just fit within the boundaries of the paper. Then draw a dot, a little smaller than the size of the tip of your little finger, in the exact center of the circle.

For the next two weeks, take five minutes out of your meditation time to concentrate on the dot within the circle (an ancient sacred symbol of Oneness). Several things may happen while doing this exercise: your eyes may want to become unfocused, you may feel tightness in your solar plexus, your attention may wander to many different thoughts, or you may begin to tell yourself, "This is a stupid exercise." Whatever happens, gently take a breath and bring your concentration back to the dot at the center of the circle. Don't expect anything—just do the exercise with the knowledge that you are building your ability to concentrate.

Active Meditation

Active meditation involves using a technique to take control of consciousness so that you can hold the mind on track. It involves actively holding something in the mind in order to control concentration, for the purpose of impressing that upon your consciousness. This kind of meditation could involve repeating certain words, sometimes in English and sometimes in Sanskrit, Arabic, Latin, or another language, in order to focus on higher realities. Active meditation also may involve focusing on your breath so that you can hold your attention and focus your mind. Holding a visualization before your mind's eye is another technique used in active meditation.

Active meditation is often easier than concentration for the beginner, because it gives you something to do with your mind rather than just asking it to be quiet. You might think of your mind as a beautiful horse that is able to carry you to incredible realms, but first it must be trained and you must learn to ride it. Active meditation will train both you and your mind over time—if you stick with your practices. If you have attempted to meditate previously, you will recognize the horse metaphor as an apt one, since the mind may be quite unruly and may not let you ride it until both you and it are ready. You might note, however, that harsh training of a horse is counterproductive. Training a horse goes much better when you make friends with the horse before you start. Giving the horse something delightful to eat improves the situation considerably; the meditation techniques you use are a bit like the carrot you might give the horse. What else does this say to a beginning meditator? Please don't beat yourself up for the inevitable thoughts that will run through your mind. Be kind to yourself. Watch the thoughts and let them go. They will gradually calm down, just as a horse that you have befriended will be more willing to accept a halter.

Active meditation may help you to attain states of altered consciousness. This is part of the reason for doing practices. By experiencing various altered states of consciousness, you begin to change some of the concepts that have been holding you back. You also will find that your view of reality will change gradually; your perspective will be that of a spiritual person, one who is guided by spiritual intentions. It is important to realize, however, that a state is only that: a temporary condition. The goal of meditation is to change your station, which is the foundation on which you build your life.

EXERCISE: ACTIVE MEDITATION

Practices using sound, such as words, are a good place to start when learning active meditation, because they require less willpower and concentration than practices that ask you to visualize. Let's begin with a practice that is wonderful because of its sound, the heart-opening "aah" sound; its meaning, "blessings"; and its effectiveness. This Sufi practice uses the phrase *Ya Faz'l* (pronounced "yah fah-zul," with the accent on the "fah"). *Ya* means roughly "Oh" or "O Thou" and serves to open the heart.

Sit quietly in the space that you have created for meditation, and begin by paying attention to your breath. Once you are relaxed, begin pronouncing the words *Ya Faz'l* over and over until you have done so thirty-three times— or ninety-nine times, if you like. (You may count on your fingers.) When you say the word *Faz'l*, you might think of your heart as a great bell or gong; the intonation of the phrase is like the ringer or the stick that strikes the gong and makes it sing. Don't rush the words; when you have finished, sit quietly for a short time and pay attention to how the repetition of this phrase has affected your consciousness and your heart. Words of power may have a major effect on you over time, so it is important to choose the words that you use wisely. This phrase, *Ya Faz'l*, attracts spiritual blessings and makes you receptive to higher consciousness; it also sets up a cycle of giving and receiving blessings. You may use this practice with confidence that it will produce only beneficial results.

Creative Imagination

Creative imagination is the stuff of the worlds that we explore in meditation. It is the content of our mind worlds, whether they are individual or collective, conscious, unconscious, or superconscious. The book *Authentic Spirituality* explains creative imagination much more fully than possible here, so you might wish to refer to that volume.

The most crucial aspect of creative imagination for our current discussion is that we have the capacity to imbue our inner worlds and mental creations with meaning and reality that is well beyond what most of us would expect. The inner worlds of your creative imagination are real and have power in your life. Working with this inner creative capacity may have a powerful impact on your physical, mental, emotional, and spiritual life.

Because of the power of your imagination, it is possible to use visualizations during meditation to affect almost any area of your life. You may use the visualizations of your creative imagination to aid the healing of your body, increase the strength of your subtle bodies, discover hidden realities, work with inner teachers, explore the universe without leaving your home, and many other time-tested activities of spiritual seekers. Much that is misunderstood about the lives of great spiritual beings relates to their mixing of the outer reality with inner experience, realms that the materialist cannot separate; to the mystic, this interpenetration of realms is natural.

When you meditate, you begin to work with the malleable inner world of creative imagination. As you grow and develop spiritually, the inner world becomes quite real, but you will not confuse the inner world with the outer, because they are different from each other in unmistakable ways.

EXERCISE: DEVELOPING YOUR CREATIVE IMAGINATION

You will no doubt notice that many of the exercises described in this book involve creative imagination. This is because most spiritual practices and meditations in some way use creative imagination as their underpinning. For the purposes of this chapter, you may experiment with the small, uncomplicated visualization that follows to become familiar with the use of creative imagination:

- Imagine yourself sitting in a beautiful pastoral setting under a beautiful tree, looking out at a meadow with a babbling brook running past you from left to right. Allow yourself to become peaceful, quiet, and relaxed.

- Let a question about your life begin to emerge into your consciousness, but do not let yourself lose your sense of peace and serenity.

- Pay attention to anything new that enters this imagined environment. If an animal, person, spirit, god, or even plant enters your pastoral surroundings, ask it what message it has for you.

- Expect an answer. The answer may come by words spoken by whoever or whatever has shown up, or by words that enter your consciousness, or by symbolic knowing what the new presence represents.

Recognize that everything that comes to you in meditation has meaning but that you should always subject your intuitions to the light of reason. Some spiritual seekers have made a shambles of their lives by failing to balance intuition with reason.

Passive Meditation

Passive meditation, which is opening the mind to intuition and deep or sublime states of consciousness, is easier for some than for others. Some people are temperamentally suited to this kind of meditation and are able to meditate this way from the very beginning with little difficulty. These people may be more intuitive than others, and to some extent, they are "born meditators." Others find that their minds are too unruly to get into a receptive mode and are not able to do passive meditation until they have developed a great deal of mental mastery. Passive meditation may involve imagery that is similar to that which you use in active mediation; the difference is that your individual will is suspended in passive meditation and you simply attempt to tune in to realities that are separate from that which you normally create. Creative imagination continues to operate, but your will is less active.

EXERCISE: PASSIVE MEDITATION

If you are new to meditation, it is hard to predict whether this exercise will be easy or challenging for you. Depending on your temperament and experience, it may be a tremendously peaceful, expansive, and revivifying experience, or you may find it a bit difficult to get into a passive space. As with all exercises in this book, just relax and do your best. There are no expectations in spiritual development—there is only the experience, along with what you learn from it.

- After doing the other practices that you have already made part of your routine, finish your period of meditation by *going into the silence.*

- Silently tell yourself that you are going into the silence at the center of all things.

- Concentrate on letting go of any thought that comes into your mind as you exhale.

- Maintain only the awareness of your breath; all other thoughts may be allowed to slip away on your exhalation.

- Picture a blank screen before your mind's eye.

- Slowly withdraw the blank screen and allow the fertile void, the vastness of consciousness, simply to be.

- After experiencing a period of true silence, you may allow thoughts to re-enter your mind; pay particular attention to what emerges first.

With practice, you may find that this "going into the silence" is one of the deepest types of spiritual experiences you ever will have. In the midst of the chaotic pace of contemporary life, you will find that you are able to access a deep well of silence, a peace that is beyond compare. Different people experience this place in somewhat different ways, and there are many levels of the reality that you touch when you sit in silence. However you experience it, this silence will nourish you and allow you to rest in the comfort of the Oneness of all being.

The next chapter, "Prayer," will explore the deeper realms of the practice of prayer. You may notice that there are similarities to the practice of meditation that we have discussed in this chapter.

twelve

Prayer

Prayer is an area that tends to be viewed in many different ways. Some people find it to be a primary means of communication with inner worlds, while others associate prayer with the regimented recitations that they endured as children. You may view it as communication with the Creator, other helpful spiritual beings, your own inner self, or in a totally different way, but whatever your approach, prayer can be a powerful spiritual practice. Some form of prayer is a spiritual practice that is virtually universal among religions and spiritual schools.

Richard is one of those who has never been all that comfortable with prayer as it is normally conceived:

> Early in my spiritual development, I saw prayer as supplication to a higher power, and that was accompanied by a sense of painful separation between myself and the Oneness that I sought. Prayer made me

feel like a child seeking blessings, guidance, or material objects from all-powerful parental figures—and that was not where I was at the time. I became much more comfortable with prayer after spending some time with Native Americans. I began to notice that my native friends often made long prayers in which they seemed to be "just talking" with the Creator. I also noticed that at formal gatherings in many native communities, it is customary to speak from your heart in order to thank those responsible for the event or others who are being honored. In my limited understanding of these cultural traditions, I began to see that there appeared to be a parallel between the sincere, heartfelt ways in which one spoke with the Creator and the ways in which one talked to the community. This awareness merged with a realization I had when talking about "ancestor worship" with an African scholar friend of mine. I suggested that *worship* was a misnomer and that *communication* with the ancestors might be a more accurate description of traditional African spirituality. My friend agreed.

Since this "aha!" experience, I have become much more comfortable with prayer. I even do it better. It is no longer a stilted "Duh . . . I don't know what to say" process, but rather a conversation with the Creator, my spiritual ancestors, or my inner self. This may suggest a historical/anthropological view of prayer, as it may have begun in tribal hunting-and-gathering societies as a way to communicate with tribal ancestors and the spirits of nature. When the peoples with patriarchal religions overran indigenous tribal lands, prayer became directed toward a more authoritarian God. In modern times, some scientifically minded people have viewed prayer as a way of communicating with the higher self. I now realize that early in my spiritual development I was overly impressed with a simplistic patriarchal view of prayer, but when I view prayer from either the ancient or modern perspective, it becomes a powerful and beautiful way of communicating with inner realities.

We will now, for a moment, switch perspectives to Jan's:

My experience with prayer has been quite different from Richard's. As a child, I found the prayerful state to be expansive and wonderful, whether I was in Nature or in a church. I remember making spontaneous little prayers of thanks when I was gazing at a flower or sitting as high as I could get on a branch of a tree in the backyard. I had a tendency to melt into Nature and to feel a glorious sense of oneness with all creation; it always left me with a deep feeling of gratitude. I never told anyone about it, as it seemed that no one would have understood. While most of the written prayers at church didn't particularly inspire me, the prayerful atmosphere did. Moments of silent prayer were often opportunities to feel a sublime presence that I interpreted as God. My own early inner prayers, generally with the themes of becoming a better person or connecting with God, were heart-felt and earnest, and I believed that they were being heard. I also related to the church prayers for people who were suffering. That sort of prayer made sense to me. Looking back, I also remember that music inspired a prayerful state in me. My father, a church organist who loved Bach above all, took me to all kinds of concerts that came to our town, and many of the musicians took me into a meditative state that seemed like prayer.

What do these different experiences suggest? What we call prayer includes a myriad of forms, and all of us have our own unique responses to the universal wish to connect with what we understand as the Divine, the One, spiritual beings, or our own inner depths. My experiences with prayer in various cultures parallel Richard's experiences with Native American peoples. I still feel in my bones the power of a Guatemalan shaman's deep prayers to "Grandmother, Grandfather," the beings of the Directions, and the Creator. Her prayers, offered as part of a long purification ceremony at an ancient Mayan sacred site, were so beautiful and soul-stirring that I cried. I felt as though I had come home after a long absence. An essential part of her prayers was giving back to the beings she invoked. Participating in the ceremony, we offered candles, incense, herbs, and sweet-smelling liquids. The prayers were effective—afterward I felt as though all of the burdens of life had fallen from my shoulders and I could face the world anew.

Pushing the rewind button on my memory tape, I am transported to saying prayers in the Catholic church in the little Colombian mountain town of Chinacota, where I lived during my time as an idealistic youth in the Peace Corps. The church was tall, and the front doors were open during Mass to let the breezes flow in—and the swallows flew in as well. What a marvel it was to look up during the long prayers to see the agile birds swooping and diving, as if to punctuate the prayers! Somehow the prayers said in Spanish touched my heart in a deep place, so I learned the "Lord's Prayer" and the "Hail Mary" prayer in that beautiful language. The "Hail Mary" prayer particularly transported me, a Protestant who at the time knew very little about the Virgin Mary. Somehow that prayer put me in touch with a feminine energy that was all-forgiving and loving—a gift, to be sure. But nothing prepared me for the first Sunday when, at the high point of the Mass, fireworks went off just outside the church doors and a community band stuck up a robust song. Surely *Dios y los santos* would pay attention to those prayers!

Other beautiful experiences in prayer took place in Bali, where Richard and I once spent an amazing summer, much of it in retreat in a sky-blue tent pitched in a grove of coconut trees overlooking the roaring Indian Ocean. The traditional Balinese way of praying includes the practice of holding a single, perfect tropical flower delicately between the fingers of both hands, which are joined in the universal hands-to-gether prayer gesture. At various points of the priest's prayer, all the kneeling people present raise their hands with the flowers in supplication and honor of the deities, whose presence is felt during the ceremonies. At the end of the ceremonies that we attended, the priest blessed each of us and gently pressed pieces of blessed rice on our foreheads and on the sides of our temples. Wearing that rice all day was a reminder of the presence of the sacred.

Walking down the narrow streets in Bodnath, the Tibetan refugee town outside Kathmandu, Nepal, ten years ago, we heard through open monastery doors the deep, deep sounding of the almost impossibly long Tibetan horns, the answering drums and cymbals, and the chanting of the monks. Having heard those wondrous sounds on CDs for years, it was like a waking dream to hear the actual live sounds. Thanks to some dear friends, we have since been privileged to have the monks of a Tibetan Buddhist monastery now located in southern India come to a city in our area several times, including one visit to the chapel at our college. It is the same every time: those sounds feel like a prayer of the deepest heart. That music, along with the deep reverence of the monks, takes me to that place where the small self melts into the Whole, and the prayer of the heart is answered by the entire universe.

There are countless ways to pray. Perhaps the most important aspect of prayer is that, to be effective, it needs to come straight from the heart, for what is prayer if it is not a call from the human heart to the Divine, to the universe, to those beings who connect with our lives? Prayer may start with rote prayers, someone else's prayers, prayers that belong to our spiritual traditions. Eventually, regardless of their origin, our prayers become our own, as they take us deeper and deeper into our beings. Prayer becomes another way to connect with the vastness and the divinity of the universe, which also exists in the depths of our own hearts. We may start out praying at a certain time, in a certain place, with a certain prayer—and gradually we find that at every time and in every place there is a prayer going in our hearts, and finally, every heartbeat and every breath becomes a prayer. When we live in constant communication with the One, our life itself is a prayer.

Knowing that there is no way to pigeonhole the world of prayer, we will discuss a few of the forms that prayer may take, such as traditional prayer, prayers for others, creative prayer, and meditative prayer.

Traditional Prayer

Many religious traditions have prayers that must be said regularly to have their desired effect, so we will label these sorts of prayer "traditional prayer." There are prayers that are to be said when waking, when retiring, and when engaging in certain daily activities, such as before eating. Some traditions, such as Islam, have established prayers that are said at specific times every day. Prayer done in this way accomplishes several purposes. All of your life becomes spiritualized when intermixed with prayer. Praying repeatedly throughout the day keeps your mind focused on transcendent principles and moderates the pull of materialism. Praying before meals reminds you to be grateful for the gift of life given by the animals and plants sacrificed for your nutrition. Richard's grandmother used to "count her blessings" every evening before bed. Counting her blessings was a prayer that thanked the Creator for all that was good in her life. Especially as she got into her eighties and nineties, she must have also seen this practice as a way of clearing her mind and conscience and preparing for death, should it come in her sleep—she was a wise woman. The psychological and spiritual worth of this practice is enormous.

Traditional prayers are usually developed by or revealed to leaders within a religion or spiritual community and then repeated by all of the followers. This may have the effect (inwardly as well as outwardly) of uniting a community toward a common purpose. Structured religious prayers such as this are useful, because everyone knows what to say, and there are usually prayers to fit all occasions. People may commit these prayers to memory and feel confident praying in public with others in the community. They may also use the prayers in private, feeling they are taking the power of their religion into the privacy of their own prayer world. Traditional prayers may lead to prayers of our own making, which then begin to look more like creative prayers.

Creative Prayer

Creative prayer is an individual's specific communication with the world of spirit. From the five-year-old child asking God to bless her parents to the elderly persons seeking a better world for their grandchildren, the creative prayer in its essence is a cry of the heart for good to triumph in life. While there is power in the traditional repetition of words that carry meaning, the spontaneous cry of the heart for good carries huge power, magnetism, and clarity.

This kind of prayer can accomplish much. Richard has had the rare opportunity to know several people whose prayers were especially effective. The first person, again, was his grandmother. People came from all over the Midwest to have his grandmother pray for their healing, and it worked. Faith healers can sometimes be seen as charlatans taking money from gullible people. Richard's grandmother always refused to take money (or anything else) from anyone she prayed for. She often said, "If I ever took money, the gift would be taken away from me." Her gift was real, her prayers were real, and the results were often stunning.

Spontaneous, creative prayer is the opening of the heart to the world beyond our senses and the communicating of a need, request, or message. It is its very spontaneity, the feeling that arises from the depths to accompany the prayer, that provides the power to communicate directly and clearly its intention.

Praying for Others

Praying for others, called intercessory prayer in some traditions, may be seen as a way of focusing energy on another person who needs assistance. Certainly there are traditions of praying for other people in many cultures. Jan thinks of the Lakota Sun Dance as one of the most powerful vehicles for praying for others that she has ever witnessed:

> The Sun Dance is a sacred ritual, so I do not suggest visiting one unless you have been invited, and if you are fortunate enough to be invited, it is important to observe carefully all of the instructions that are given to you. Everything is done in a traditional way, and everyone present needs to honor these traditions to preserve the sacredness of the ceremony and the safety of the dancers. The sun dancers, who commit themselves to terrific self-sacrifice for the benefit of relatives, friends, an entire group, or even beyond, become living prayers. Those watching from under the shaded arbors surrounding the Sun Dance area are not just observers—everyone participates and contributes to the ritual in some way. During a Sun Dance to which I was invited, those of us under the arbors prayed and danced quietly in place to give strength to the dancers. It was one of the holiest ceremonies I have ever experienced; I felt a powerful presence of the Sacred. The sacred cottonwood tree in the center of the Sun Dance area became, in my mind, the sacred pole of the entire earth, and the dancers were blessing this beautiful and vulner-

able planet. I don't know whether my experience was shared by anyone else, but it doesn't matter. What I saw confirmed for me that the Sun Dance is at one level a powerful prayer that benefits all of us.

Some of you may have a calling to pray for others. Many cultures have individuals whose work it is to pray for those who ask, and sometimes just for those who are in need. It's beautiful work, yet there are guidelines to consider. If we believe that prayer can be effective, then we must ask if praying for others, unless they ask us to do so, is meddling in their lives. This is a question that all must answer for themselves, but we will offer a couple of thoughts. Generally, praying for others' well-being is a lovely practice and can only lead to good. If, however, someone is seriously ill, one cannot know for certain what that person's deepest wish may be, and it is extremely important to respect all persons' right to choose their own destinies. In such a case, we feel it is best not to pray for such a person's healing—although one may pray for blessings for the individual—unless the person asks for healing prayers. It is all right to ask the person if they would like your prayers, but then it's important to do as they request. The main exceptions we see are that a mother or father can generally speak for a child. You may see that this is complex, and we can touch only the surface of the issue here. A similar situation might be when a person is trying to decide what course of action to take in life. Again, to pray for the person to take a particular path might be considered a violation of that person's right to make choices.

Given these limitations, praying for others can be one of the most fulfilling kinds of prayer. Jan usually ends her morning meditations by praying for the entire planet and all beings, and she is often struck by the way in which these prayers make her feel so joyful. Forgetting the small self, even through prayer, may lead to great joy, for we are letting go of whatever holds us down.

Meditative Prayer

Meditative prayer is our term for the deep spiritual experience that may evolve from other forms of prayer. There is a growing body of literature about meditative prayer from a Christian perspective. Much of this has been written by contemplatives and mystics who have experienced that after an intense period of more traditional prayer, they feel a sense of release into the vastness, a communion with God, a profound connectedness with all life, or a complete loss of self in the Oneness. The experience may come as a surprise, as the doctrine these contemplatives have been taught may not have prepared them for the actual experience. The Sufis teach that after repeating sacred phrases—a form of prayer in our view—you may simply sit in silence and allow the energy of the practice to permeate your being. If the practice has been deep and true, the silence may be profound. The early Christian desert fathers, who usually lived in remote monasteries and wandered the Middle Eastern deserts, believed in "praying without ceasing." One version of their most famous prayer, the "Jesus Prayer," went like this: "Lord Jesus Christ, have mercy on me . . ."

The goal was to keep this prayer going all the time, until it totally transformed the consciousness. Many other traditions around the globe have similar sorts of practices, which is not surprising, since we know that the human mind and heart respond in the same ways to certain stimuli, regardless of the specifics of the spiritual path. Intense, heartfelt prayer, whatever the form, may lead you to a place of deep inner silence, where the world stops and infinity begins—at least for a while.

Exercise: Creating Your Own Prayers

In this exercise, you are going to have an opportunity to create a prayer that could become a part of your daily practice. Before developing a prayer, it is good to allow yourself time to get into a deep space.

- Find a quiet spot in Nature or in a corner of your home. Some people find that lighting a candle or burning incense helps them to focus, while for others, this is a distraction. Do whatever works for you. Remember that this is a time when you may let the rest of the world go and simply be present in the moment. You might think of yourself as a drop of water or a wave in the ocean that is God, the One, or the Universal Mind.

- After you have quieted your mind, contemplate your life and what you care about most. What emerges may be the beginning of your prayer, your communication with that which is larger than you are. The object of your prayer depends on your own perspective.

It may be called God, the Creator, a saint, guardian angels, or even archangels, spirits, the great Oneness, or a spiritual being to whom you relate.

- Let your mind settle into your heart center. This may sound strange, but many traditions recognize that the heart and mind work best in combination, and some consider the mind to be just the covering of the heart. As you become quiet, you will gradually find that you can feel your heart center more easily. Thinking briefly of someone you love may help you to get in touch with the heart.

- Let your prayer come out of this space. There may be words, or the prayer may be simply a feeling of connection with the One. If there are words, you may let them flow, or you may wish to remember them for another time.

- When the prayer time is almost over, express your gratitude for the opportunity to connect with whatever being your prayer was related to. Gratitude is one of the most beneficial emotions; at the very least, it enlarges your heart and makes you receptive. Most spiritual traditions suggest that gratitude opens the way for great blessings.

- Finally, the observation that there is a pattern to the universe may help to increase your faith in life—not easy in times like the present, to be sure. What we hope for may or may not be in alignment with this hidden universal pattern, which some may call "the will of God" or "the cause behind the cause." Sometimes acknowledging that we don't see the entire picture and bowing to the higher will is a useful way to end a prayer. In her life, whenever Jan remembers to surrender to the higher will, her life opens up and blockages disappear—or she sees their higher purpose.

- You might try to remember this space and perhaps even the words of your prayer, if it seems appropriate, and say this or another prayer every morning before you get out of bed and every evening before you lie down. In this way, prayer—communion with something vaster than yourself—will become your first and last acts of each day. You will find that gradually your entire day will become infused with spirituality.

thirteen

Connecting with Nature

Becoming aware of our connections with the exquisite web of life to which we all belong is one of the most natural ways to grow spiritually. Most of us have since childhood experienced those moments when we feel one with a flower, a tree, an animal, a glorious landscape, the stars in the night sky, or even the entirety of creation. We treasure these moments as islands of sanity in the rush of our lives. Some of us walk in the wilderness, hike, camp, or climb mountains in order to experience again this revivifying connectedness. Jan remembers the first time that she felt this in an overwhelming way as an adult:

> I was setting up my tent for a retreat in a wilderness area in the mountains of northern New Mexico, and night fell suddenly—or perhaps I was so intent on getting my tent staked out that I didn't notice until

I looked up and realized that the sky was dark, except for the myriad of bright stars. As I gazed into the sky, something shifted, and I somehow *knew* that the stars were all interconnected—they were calling out to each other. It was as if I could *see* the invisible threads that held them all together. Then I realized that they were calling out to the tall pine trees that surrounded me, and the pine trees were calling out to each other and to the stars. The entire universe was a vibrating, loving, interconnected One, and I was melting into it. All of us, the stars, the trees, we humans, and all of creation were One Being, and at that moment, all were shining and loving. Love *is* the glue that holds everything together.

That moment is almost as alive in my mind today as it was that night many years ago, even though I've been gifted with similar moments since then. Now I feel that connectedness when I'm working in my garden or when I walk out on the deck at night and feel the breezes caress my face as the frogs in the little creek in the nearby ravine croak their funny chorus. Last night, the whippoorwill was carrying on loudly and insistently, his song punctuated by the occasional hoot of an owl, all of it made sweeter by the perfume of the blooming linden tree and the twinkling of the fireflies in the grasses.

What does Jan's story have to do with spiritual development? It seems that the vibrant world of Nature is full of beings, some of whom long for us to acknowledge our connectedness. They are willing to teach us about the nature of the universe, to help us to understand that we are at home in the natural world. So many of us have grown up alienated from our home as part of that world. Our lives might not be so frenetic if we could allow ourselves to relax into the beauty and the consciousness of this planet.

Clarissa Pinkola Estés retells the powerful story of the seal woman who is captured by a fisherman who takes her home to be his wife. After performing her duties as wife and mother for many years, she begins to dry up. Her skin dries, her hair falls out, her eyes dim, and she can hardly bear the pain, both emotional and physical, of living so far from her sea home. At last, in desperation, she takes her young son and escapes back to the sea (Estés 1992, 258–262). How many of us live in similar circumstances, constantly telling ourselves to be brave, to buck up, that we can do it? We may beat ourselves up for not being able to handle the constant demands of life in a contemporary society, yet it may not be that *we* are lacking—perhaps the entire social milieu is an assault upon our ability to be truly human.

While we spoke of the patterns through which life teaches us in the previous chapter, some traditional indigenous people carry teachings that bear witness to a profound connectedness that goes far beyond the experience of most of us. Jan's visits to people who live in native cultures have been healing, a remedy for dealing with the stress of modern life:

Much as I love my job, I find that even relatively brief visits to Mayan people in Guatemala and indigenous communities in the U.S. have been a release from the belief that I should be able to "do it all," although sometimes it is difficult to remember this back at home when working at my day job, teaching in a small college. My visits bring the world back into focus again, and I *remember* a reality of deep, deep connectedness and profound knowing that is, I believe, our human heritage, long lost to so many.

Participating in a Mayan ceremony led by a shaman in an ancient place beneath an old, old tree a few years ago, I felt the burdens of my life melting off my back as I was enveloped in a powerful yet compassionate world of beings. The ceremony, which had some commonalities with the Lakota rituals in which I've been privileged to participate, invoked the presence of so many beings that the atmosphere was charged with wonder and energy. I would not presume to try to explain the power of the ceremony. The shaman had trained for years and years to learn the rituals and to develop the capacity to connect with the forces that she invoked. Yet I do know from meeting with her and other Mayan shamans that the world they live in is exquisitely complex and ordered. Virtually nothing happens by chance.

Our job as humans is, in part, to learn our places and our roles in this beautiful, rich, wonderful drama of life. When we develop the humility to learn our places and our work, which are often not nearly as important as we like to think they are, we may experience the deep joy of knowing that we are at home in this world, that this amazing life on this planet is a gift beyond measure.

How might we practice connecting with the web of life in the midst of the situations in which most of us find ourselves? It seems interesting that as our environment is increasingly degraded, as many of our cities and even our rural areas are becoming less and less pleasant because of air and water pollution, traffic congestion, and lack of green spaces, many people are becoming interested in organic gardening, recycling, and other forms of taking care of the environment. Here are some possible activities for connecting with the natural world:

- Teach a child how to grow plants from seeds, even in the house in little containers. Tell the child about how seeds turn into little plants and how to take care of them, and watch the child's sense of wonder take off.

- Start a miniature garden on your patio or deck or in your backyard. Enjoy eating fresh food from your own little garden.

- Visit a local farmers' market and talk with the growers about their lives and their gardens and farms, and learn what their work means to them.

- Grow plants (without pesticides) that butterflies and hummingbirds like, such as butterfly bushes, coral bells, salvias, lilies, honeysuckle, echinacea, and almost any plant with a sweet aroma.

- Install bird feeders, including hummingbird feeders (if hummingbirds come to your area), and keep them full all year, if possible, as birds will come to depend on you.

- Go walking or hiking wherever you can find trails, even in urban areas. Walk at your own speed, but take time to rest and hang out with the natural world that you encounter. You may meet deer, foxes, birds, and more!

- Give yourself permission to spend time hanging out in a botanical garden or a wildlife refuge—or just your own backyard. Look at the amazing colors of the flowers and inhale their scents, and watch for the eagles or whatever wildlife is present. They may touch your heart or connect with your mind in a totally unexpected way.

- Start a journal in which you write about your experiences with the natural world. Chances are that you will become more attentive when you know you will be writing about what you see.

- Sit down under a tree, with your back rested against its trunk, and tune in to the life force in the tree. Leave a little symbolic gift for the tree, such as a little of your food, some cornmeal, or some pure tobacco.

- Find the most untouched wild spot you can locate, and, if it seems appropriate, sit there for a time and just observe what happens there. Even ants or caterpillars may sometimes behave in surprising ways that seem to carry messages to you—if you are open to the possibility.

- Visit a mountain stream, if possible, or else the clearest stream you can find, and listen very carefully to the music of the stream. After positioning yourself so that the current of the stream runs in front of you from left to right, visualize the cleansing energy of the stream flowing through your being, washing out the old energy and revitalizing you with the freshness of the stream.

- Give back to Nature whenever you can. Leave little symbolic offerings when you are touched by a flower or when anything in the natural world helps you to feel a deep relationship with that world. What matters is your recognition of the life that exists in all of Nature, as well as your intention to give back. (We humans tend to be "takers" rather than "givers," so far as our relationship with Nature is concerned, so it is helpful to start to change that pattern.)

Sacred Places

Some places in the natural world feel more sacred and powerful than others. These are places where you may go to attune to special energies that may be healing, uplifting, energizing, or consciousness-raising—or all of the above. We hesitate to write about these places, as they are so vulnerable in a world that often lacks understanding of their value and their need for protection. Still, many sacred places have helped us in our journeys, and we suggest that you seek out such sites if you feel attracted by the possibility. Chances are that there is a sacred place not too far from where you live, and you might be able to arrange a visit. The most important thing to do before visiting such a location is to prepare yourself to enter with humility and respect so that you will be able to feel the energies of the place and so that your presence will not be jarring to the place or to others who are there. Reading about what others have experienced in the place can be helpful as well, but it is important not to expect that you will have the same experience that other people have had. Your experience will be unique.

We will mention a few places that have been meaningful for us. The most wonderful places for you, however, may be the places that you find on your own. There are so many lovely places that few people know about, and if you stay alert, you will find some of them. One word of caution: many such places are known to local indigenous peoples, such as the Native American nations of the United States and the First Nations peoples of Canada, and these groups have their own special ways of relating to sacred places. Often there are ritual ways of showing respect; sacred places are used for prayer, vision quests, and other important functions. If you enter such a spot, it is important to stop at a natural boundary and inwardly ask the spirits of the place for permission to enter. A friend of ours who is a Navajo medicine man told us years ago that a good practice is to pick up a little soil, hold it in your hand, and tell the spirits that you come in peace. We have followed his advice and found that it leads to a harmonious experience. Usually one can inwardly sense an answer, and once in a while, the answer is more tangible. When we were visiting the exquisite Mesa Verde "ruins," the ancient cliff dwellings that were home to the ancestral peoples of the Southwest, Richard picked up a few small rocks to ask permission to enter. Because there were many people around, he asked inwardly, and immediately a lovely yellow butterfly appeared and rested on his hand. It felt like a tender affirmation.

If there happen to be people at the place you visit who are conducting a ceremony, a vision quest, or another ritual when you arrive, you will, of course, need to postpone your visit. Having nonmembers of the group enter the space during a ceremony may have a seriously disruptive effect on the event. If you wonder about the advisability of visiting a sacred place that seems to be in the territory (such as a reservation or a pueblo) of an indigenous group, protocol calls for finding a tribal leader, a medicine person, or someone else who has some authority to ask—with respect and humility—for permission to visit. Following these suggestions will make it much more likely that you will be a welcome visitor and that you will have a good experience.

By now, you may be asking where you might find such sacred spots. You can probably guess that natural places of beauty are often sacred and powerful. Mountains, hills, streams, waterfalls, large rocks, and old trees may be special places. There are great differences among such places, however, as Jan has discovered:

Once, I had the opportunity to jump into the sacred Ganges River in northern India near Rishikesh, where the great river was rushing down from its high mountain source. At that place, the Ganges was absolutely clear, it was frigid, and it was flowing so fast that a friend and I took turns getting into the shoulder-deep water. Each of us held on to the one in the river in turn, and even then it felt as though we might have been swept away. At the time, I was a bit skeptical about the reality of sacred places, so I was not expecting anything; it just seemed like the thing to do. Amazingly enough, my consciousness made a leap after the experience, although one might explain this away as being the result of the ice-cold water on the brain!

To move to an experience a little closer to home, as a child my favorite place was located at a bend of the little stream that flowed through my grandparents' farm in the loess hills of northwestern Iowa. Graceful weeping willows bent over the stream at that spot, and there was a special tree that leaned over the water so that I could perch on it, right above the water. At the time, I knew nothing about sacred places, but I felt good there in that peaceful place. Usually, I climbed the nearby windmill (supposedly off-limits) so that I could see as far as I could see, and then I would walk down to the stream and sit there on the friendly willow as long as I could before being missed. It was a child's paradise. What is the difference between a "feel-good" place and a sacred place? That is a matter of experience, although there are a few factors that may enhance the energy of a place. One of them is that there may be a natural place where energy can accumulate, such as the bend of that little stream.

Other places where we have had glimpses of the sacred include the Teton Mountains in Wyoming; the red rocks of northern Arizona; the Himalayas near Pokara, Nepal; many Native American reservations, where the natural energies are less disturbed; certain ancient places in the Southwest of the U.S.; and beaches from Oregon to Bali where the ocean comes roaring in. Many churches and temples in Latin America and Europe were built where indigenous people once found sacred natural places, and the more recently built structures have benefited from the energies. You still may feel the power of such places. While we could name countless other locations, our goal here is to inspire you to find your own places. Your intention and perhaps a little research will take you to them.

Nature, Dreams, Visions, and Spirit Animals

Have you ever had a dream about a special place or perhaps an especially alive animal? If so, it probably caught your attention—and with good reason. Sometimes your inner self speaks to you through dreams, and it may use the natural world and the beings that populate it to try to communicate. We have been lucky to have had many such dreams, and at first we had to learn how to interpret them.

(Please see chapter 14, "Dreams," for more information.) One of the first such dreams that Jan remembers seemed to carry a message about taking care of Nature:

> My young sons and I were visiting my sister on the coast of Oregon, where Nature is alive, with enthusiastic vegetation growing everywhere and the Pacific Ocean roaring not far away. The second night there, I dreamed that I was climbing up a small mountain that clearly had been covered with green vegetation at one time. Now the mountain was suffering under the heavy, unthinking pounding of the boot-clad feet of many hikers. I looked around me, and there were a number of people trudging up the mountain with me, and all of them were cutting into the precious soil with no awareness of what they were doing to the little green that was left. In the dream, I could actually *feel* the excruciating pain of the earth. Then the dream shifted to another time—but on the same mountain. In this part of the dream, I was leading a group of gentle people on a narrow trail up the mountain, and this time the mountain had recovered and was again lush and green and peaceful. All of us were tuned in to the earth, and we were walking so carefully, as though we were consciously blessing the earth with our feet. When we reached the crest of the mountain, there was a huge, beautiful bell suspended from an arch, sending out exquisite, resonating tones in all directions. Peace and happiness were in the air.

You might ask whether this dream might be interpreted on a psychological level rather than a spiritual level. Actually, many dreams may be interpreted on multiple levels, and each of these levels holds its own truth for us. The answer to this question, then, is that this dream did hold significant psychological meaning for Jan, and it also carried a spiritual message. Another dream of Jan's that might be seen similarly was one that also struck her as having a powerful meaning. It came at a time in her life when she was working hard, putting in long hours writing most of a three-volume document to keep our academic program accredited:

Richard and I took a weekend break and drove to Kansas City, where we visited the wonderful Nelson Art Museum. (Often, visiting an art museum or listening to a great concert will provide new images and new connections for the mind.) That night, a beautiful dream came to me, and this time the connection with Nature was a gorgeous white owl, whose wingspan was enormous. In the dream, I was again trudging up a mountain, but this time I was climbing at night with only the moonlight to illumine the way. I felt a powerful presence overhead and looked up to see a magnificent snow-white owl with perhaps a twenty-foot wingspan swooping low above me. The owl had a message: "It's time to climb the mountain by night."

I woke up immediately. It was as if the owl were still in the room, and I had to know what she was trying to tell me. Richard and I help each other out with our dreams, and I was especially glad that he was there for this one, as owls for some cultures symbolize loss or death, as well as the more common attribute of wisdom. Neither seemed to be the case in this dream. On one level, the lovely white owl was telling me that it was time to pay more attention to the feminine side of my life, to learn more about feminine aspects of spirituality. Owls tend to be seen as feminine symbols, and this one certainly was feminine, just as mountains for me generally symbolize spiritual heights. I was overemphasizing the masculine side of my being by working so hard, and it was time to seek a balance. A being from the natural world had come to bear the message.

Sometimes animals come in visions when meditating or when making a shamanic journey. You might be interested to know that in the Lakota (Sioux) language, as well as in many other Native American languages, according to native friends of ours, there is no corresponding word for *animal*. In Lakota, one speaks of "the deer nation," "the bear nation," and "the bison nation," or sometimes "the deer people," and so on. This terminology connotes so much more respect than the word *animal* does, and learning this perspective has helped us to understand more clearly the important role of all beings in the web of life. When a member of the deer nation, for example, comes to Jan, she gives it even more significance than she might have previously. She shares one such experience:

Once, when camping at a spiritual seminar with my two young sons, a great thunderstorm came up in the late afternoon. We were in the tent instead of attending the seminar, because my nine-year-old son had an earache, unusual for him. The storm was so powerful that we had to hang on to the inside poles of our tent to keep it from blowing away, and to keep my sons (and myself!) from getting scared, I taught them every silly camp song I could remember from my high school days as a camp counselor. We actually had a good time and ended up in high spirits.

Following the storm, the setting sun shed a glorious golden glow on the forest landscape surrounding us, and out of that glow emerged a huge stag; his coat was a luminous reddish-brown color. My older son saw him first and whispered an amazed "Look!" to us. The stag, with his many-pronged antlers, walked serenely up to within perhaps eight feet of the tent, and then we realized that this was no ordinary stag. He appeared to be a spirit animal, seemingly not flesh at all, and his energy was both loving and mesmerizing. All three of us were filled with awe as we gazed at this magnificent being, who somehow seemed to be there to encourage us. After what seemed to be a long time, the stag slowly turned and walked back into the forest, leaving my sons and me in the afterglow. We sat in silence for a while, and then, with few words, decided it was time to sleep. My younger son said, "Mom, my earache is gone!"

At the time of the spirit deer's appearance, I knew little about such things, and neither did I know that thunderstorms, to traditional Lakota and others, are often considered to be manifestations of the Thunderbeings, powerful beings that inhabit the West and bring the blessings of rain and possible transformation with them.

You do not have to hang out with native peoples to learn to understand the messages that Nature sends. Jan has been blessed with many friends from various tribal nations, who have generously taught her so much, and she is tremendously grateful. Native peoples, however, wish to preserve their own cultures, and large numbers of non-natives coming to them for knowledge can be overwhelming and invasive. What we suggest is that all of us have the capacity to connect with the natural world—we simply need to slow down and pay attention. Nature is eager to communicate with us!

fourteen

Dreams

One of the most useful tools for your psychological and spiritual growth may be your dreams. Most spiritual guides that we have known find working with the dreams of those they are guiding extremely useful, because dreams are windows into what is really happening inwardly, unfiltered by the conscious mind. When you recognize that a large portion of spiritual development relates to shining the light of consciousness on that of which you are not aware, you realize that what you think you are is only a very small portion of what you fully *are* at any given point. The same is true for the world around you. All of us are aware of only a small portion of what truly exists. Dreams, which Freud called the "royal road to the unconscious," can give you a peek at what lies beneath or beyond your awareness.

This is also one of the areas where the line between psychological and spiritual realms blurs. It would be far better if we did not expect there to be a line at all, except that too often the spiritual gets trivialized or gobbled up by a culture that wishes to make everything psychological. Mythology, mysticism, and spiritual development are older and more comprehensive systems of psychology than our very young scientific system. With this perspective as a given, we might seek a synthesis of ancient and modern wisdom. In such a system, interpretation of dreams would play a major role.

Types of Dreamers

Some people remember dreams almost every night. Other people hardly ever remember dreams. Some people have very vivid and detailed dreams, while others typically remember only vague and sketchy dreams. For some, the norm is to dream long and complicated story lines, while others dream quick snippets. Some people's dreams contain much violent or seemingly bizarre material, and others' may seem very mundane. It is important not to judge your ability to benefit from dream work based on what your dreams have been like in the past. What is important is what will unfold; once you begin to work with dreams, you will learn to start with your dreams as they are.

Even though your dreams may typically be of one sort, it is probable that as you work with your dreams, you will occasionally begin to experience atypical dreams. A few years ago, Richard taught a college class on dreams. The class became very powerful, and the way many people in the class dreamed changed. Some of the students in the class who usually remembered vivid dreams began not to remember their dreams at all. Others who seldom remembered dreams began to recall them. A few people who usually didn't have nightmares had one, as the barriers to the unconscious lifted, and some who had many nightmares began having more peaceful dreams. It is common at times when you become deeply immersed in the world of symbolism and the unconscious that your dreams will change; your unconscious mind will seek unique means to speak to you.

Types of Dreams

Dreams can take many forms, and some dreams have deeper significance than others. For the purpose of this discussion, we will categorize dreams as follows:

- Taking-out-the-garbage dreams
- Mundane psychological dreams
- Psychological/spiritual dreams
- Deep spiritual dreams

The first two types of dreams we will discuss only briefly, because they have less relevance to the topic of this book, but the third and fourth types we will consider more fully, because they are extremely useful in the process of spiritual growth.

Taking-out-the-garbage dreams are simply the brain processing the events of the day. A bit like an eidetic image that is seen with the eyes closed, these "garbage" dreams have no particular meaning or purpose except to clear out the images and experiences of the previous day. We typically don't remember these dreams, and they often happen during the REM periods early in the sleep period.

Mundane psychological dreams are very useful dreams for interpreting and dealing with psychological issues, dilemmas, and traumas. Some of these dreams occur as nightmares, and some in a less traumatic fashion. When you were a child, you may have dreamed about giants, witches, or monsters. These are typical ways of processing good-parent/bad-parent dilemmas in the symbols of childhood. As you get older, you may dream of running from something but being unable to move, while in waking life you are feeling thwarted or struggling with difficult choices. You may dream about fires closing in on you during a time of rapid change in your life. You may dream about losing your teeth when you feel unable to accomplish your goals. These and countless other dream scenarios are common in our psychological lives and may, if we pay attention to them, let us know what we fear or what we are struggling with.

The majority of dreams that we remember will be psychological dreams of this mundane sort. If we pay attention to them, we can grow to understand our psychological nature without necessarily having to go into therapy. We should never dismiss them as merely psychological, because without a solid psychological base, much of our spiritual pursuit can degenerate into a spiritual bypass of our psychological issues. Psychological dreams can warn us of problems with which we are struggling, but they can also alert us to opportunities for growth. As we begin to talk about opportunities, we enter a realm in which psychological/spiritual dreams are more common.

Let's explore a brief caveat. Most dreams may have meaning on at least two of the levels we have mentioned, and often three. Just as myths, fairy tales, and other symbolic stories can be understood on multiple levels, dreams may also be approached on different levels of meaning. The categorization that we are presenting is necessarily artificial and is only an attempt to clarify levels of dreaming. In reality, dreams are multidimensional explorations of our psyche and cannot be limited to categories.

The *psychological/spiritual dream* is more likely than the mundane psychological dream to point to growth and opportunity, but this is not the primary difference. In essence, the main difference involves the issue that is being addressed by the dream and the primary focus that you are addressing at that point in your life. For instance, Richard has often had dreams involving water:

> I have had many dreams about water, particularly never-ending oceans, lakes that are flooding, bridges that must be crossed but are nearly washed out—in other words, dreams where I was in danger of being overwhelmed by water. At one point in my early twenties, this dream related to being overwhelmed by my emotions. At another point in my life, it related to psychological work I was doing that was bringing me closer to unconscious material I had been avoiding. At a still later time in my life, these dreams related to the task of finding the feminine within. It

is quite possible that before I die these dreams will again emerge, as I deal with being a wave (an individual) that is receding again into the ocean of being (death). To clarify where I would place these dreams, the first instance fits within the mundane, the second is related to both the mundane and the spiritual, and the third is more spiritual than mundane, because the inner marriage of the masculine and feminine represents important spiritual work.

Psychological/spiritual dreams have the purpose of pointing out the spiritual work that we have done, the work we are doing, and the work we are approaching. In the previous chapter, "Connecting with Nature," Jan shared several experiences that illustrate crucial spiritual transitions that were announced by a dream. An example from Richard's life also illustrates this level of dreaming, as well as the reality that dreams may have meaning at many levels at once:

I had a recurring dream for many years that I was walking through a zoo and came to a large gymnasium. Once in the gym, I noticed a beautiful, large jungle animal at the top of the bleachers. It came loping down toward me, and I was frightened. The first several times that I had the dream, I would wake up at this point. Over the years, I stayed asleep until the animal reached me and lunged for me, and then I would wake up. Finally, the last time I had the dream, this magnificent animal leaped on me, but rather than eating me, we merged—he was within me. Several years later, when I began doing shamanic work, it was that very being that was waiting for me as my power animal.

It is clear that there are many meanings to this dream. Becoming comfortable with, owning, and eventually mastering both his physical nature and his power were major psychological and spiritual issues with which Richard had to deal. The progression of the recurring dream was a barometer of his inner progress, and in a way, it also foretold the future. As anyone who has worked closely with a power animal may tell you, such beings are very real in inner realms, just not in the physical world. To have met and worked to incorporate this being and his qualities for over thirty years prior to developing a conscious working relationship with him was an incredible gift for Richard.

Sometimes psychological/spiritual dreams have an element of humor. Jan had a rather humorous yet significant series of dreams early on her spiritual path:

These dreams came as I was trying to find a way to live my spirituality in the world. In the dreams, I was always trying to climb a mountain or achieve some other difficult physical feat in the world, and I never could find the right shoes for the journey. In the first such dream, the only shoes I could find were a pair of beautiful but flimsy slippers. Even in the dream, this struck me as rather humorous. I searched and searched among the various pairs of boots and hiking shoes that were scattered around the trail, but none fit, or else I could find only one shoe of a pair. I finally started out up the mountain in my ridiculous slippers; they were totally inadequate for the journey, but I climbed that mountain anyway.

There are multiple levels to this dream, but on one level, this is the way many of us feel about our spiritual journeys. We fear that we don't have "the right stuff" to make the journey—and we seldom have exactly what we think we need. We feel inadequate, and yet we climb the mountain anyway, making the best of circumstances and our own limitations. Interestingly enough, after many such challenging dream journeys, Jan finally had a dream in which she found the perfect shoes for the trip!

Deep spiritual dreams usually are striking in their clarity and vividness. They often carry a sense of the numinous, as though something of extraordinary beauty and meaning has come into your life. When you awaken from such dreams, you may even feel slightly disoriented for a moment or two, yet you also may feel as though something tremendously important has happened. This is the moment to write down your dream so that you will be able to work on it later. What do you make of dreams that seem powerful and important but carry a negative tone? You may find it comforting to know that some of the most significant spiritual dreams may come in pairs—a positive dream and a negative dream. Most often, the negative dream comes first and might be interpreted as a tool for going deep, dealing with, and clearing out negative energies in preparation for the beautiful dream and its message.

Some deep spiritual dreams give us a glimpse of something to come. Some people with psychic temperaments will dream about events that will transpire for themselves, for others, or for groups of people. Many who have these dreams have no idea what to make of them, and so they dismiss them or forget them. Some who have prophetic dreams learn to trust them and occasionally share them when appropriate. While this type of dream is important—and may be distressing—often it is based on temperament or extreme need and is not really all that useful for spiritual development. It is the rare and powerful dream that tells us of our own future, usually in a symbolic way, that is important for spiritual development. Let's look at two examples, one fairly straightforward and the other more symbolic, that illustrate what we mean by a deep spiritual dream. First is an example from Richard:

> I once dreamed that I had crossed a large body of water in a small boat and came ashore on an island. There to greet me was a white-haired man with a small beard, a powerful chest, and a big smile. He greeted me with the words, "Welcome, I have been waiting for you, and I will introduce you to the Ancient Ones." That was the end of the dream. I have remembered this dream often in the twenty-five years since it occurred and have come to think that the man was a potential myself and that, after a particularly important step in my life, he was welcoming me on to the path toward becoming him.

Some kinds of deep spiritual dreams may serve as initiations, signifying the beginning of a major transition in your spiritual life. They also may tell you symbolically what the next step is on your path, and sometimes they may show you how far you have come. The latter sort of dreams may come in a series that occurs over a period of years, each with some modification on the previous dreams. So, a second, more symbolic example of a deep spiritual dream would be a series of dreams of a house that changes with each dream. A house often signifies a person's self in a dream, and when the dream house becomes larger, more translucent, and more light-filled, it might indicate that your being is becoming larger, more translucent, and more light-filled. These types of dreams are best kept to yourself, for sharing these dreams with anyone except a trusted spiritual friend or teacher may drain some of the spiritual energy associated with the dream. You will find, however, that these are dreams that you will never forget, for they are important landmarks in your spiritual development and are as real as significant events in your outer life.

A special example of this sort of dream might be the reassuring dreams that people occasionally have before death. Jan's mother, a devout and open-minded Christian, had a beautiful dream about two weeks before she died at the age of ninety-two. In her vivid dream, she heard a tremendous choir singing an old church hymn that began with the phrase, "Up from the grave He arose!" The hymn was about Christ's resurrection and life after death. Above the stirring singing of the choir, Jan's mother heard clearly the booming baritone voice of her beloved father, who had sung for all their little country church's weddings, funerals, and special celebrations. The dream was so powerful that when we visited her the next day, she was still glowing from the joy of it, and she exclaimed, "Now I know for sure that I'll be OK! I'm not afraid in the least anymore." And indeed she was OK. A few hours before her peaceful transition to the next worlds, she told Richard, "You know, the only bad part of this dying thing is that I'll never know how many home runs Sammy Sosa hits this year!"

Exercise: Keeping a Dream Journal

A good way to start working with your dreams is to begin a dream journal. Buy a notebook of some sort and keep it and a pen next to your bed. Then train yourself so that immediately upon waking, you take your notebook and record what you remember of your dreams. You will find it easiest to remember a dream if you wake abruptly after the dream; this is more common with strong and psychologically important dreams. Dreams that you have in the morning just before you wake are likely to be more psychologically significant, as are dreams that you have during a short nap.

Try not to have expectations that you will have certain powerful spiritual dreams. Instead, accept whatever dreams you remember as gifts to be treasured, gifts that provide insights into your inner being. Do not discount psychological dreams; they are as important to your spiritual development as prophetic dreams—maybe more important.

Knowledge of your psychological issues grounds you in reality and keeps you from becoming ego-inflated or pursuing spiritual solutions for psychological needs. If you are like most of us, you might have five or ten deep spiritual dreams in your life, but you will have thousands of important psychological dreams. Use these psychological dreams to help you to create a personality that is prepared for and receptive to spiritual realities.

Here are some hints for working with the dreams that you journal:

Guidelines for Dream Interpretation

- While there are different ways to work with psychological dreams, you may want to start with the easiest approach. See everything in the dream as a part of you. Evaluate the message of the dream by thinking of all of the players in the dream—even natural and inanimate objects—as aspects of yourself working out issues internally.

- Avoid obvious, literal interpretations, such as interpreting a dream about arguing with your best friend as having a problem with your best friend. Instead, ask yourself, "Which of my qualities does my best friend represent, and how might I be in conflict with that quality?"

- Do not interpret a sexual dream as literally sexual. Instead, view it as some sort of deep relationship with the quality represented by the person whom you are involved with in the dream.

- You can buy a book on dream symbolism and use it as a guide, but when the book's interpretation differs from your intuition of what the symbolism means for you, trust your own intuition.

- Keep an eye out for core issues, such as the emergence of masculine/feminine growth issues, journey (path) themes, and signals of a major change in your life.

By following these guidelines, you will find that your dreams will most likely come alive for you. They have the potential to become a major source of inspiration and guidance to you as your inner life develops, and you may even start to look forward to each night's sleep as a door to new realities.

fifteen

Becoming a Whole Person

A primary goal of spiritual development is becoming a whole person. If you search the hidden depths of virtually any fully developed spiritual path, within you will find knowledge regarding the quest to reconcile the opposites of life. One pair of these opposites may be called *yang* and *yin*, *jelal* and *jemal*, spirit and soul, or masculine and feminine. There are some cultural differences among these concepts, but for the most part they refer to the same phenomena, sometimes called the right and left hands of God. They relate respectively to the active, creating, doing parts of our beings and the passive, receiving, and reflective parts.

These polarities are not confined to the genders with which they are most commonly associated, but rather they are inherent capacities within all people. The biological nature of our bodies, societal gender roles, and the roles we assume because of sexual orientation may affect our starting points, but the goal is the same for all: the full experience of our human potential. One of the purposes of conscious spiritual development is to accelerate the process of becoming a whole human being. Being *whole* means having full access to all of your potential, not just that which has been assigned to you by your culture as a result of your reproductive equipment. The chart below gives an overview of the process that we will be describing.

Inner Reconciliation of Masculine/Feminine Polarities

BEGINNING STAGE	DISCOVERY STAGE	RECONCILIATION STAGE	COMPLETION STAGE
Pseudomasculine or Pseudofeminine	*Feminization or Masculinization*	*True Masculine or True Feminine*	*Wholeness*
Rigid stereotypical roles based on cultural restrictions for men and women. Often rejecting and oppressing toward external and internal opposite polarity.	Discovery and development of qualities of the opposite polarity within.	Discovery of a same-sex, authentic, nonstereotypical polarity within.	Achievement of access to all of one's potential rather than only a culturally limited gender stereotype. Accepting of polarities wherever found.

This chart provides a simple outline of a process that has been part of spiritual development in virtually every part of the world for thousands of years. It provides a typical sequence, but it should not be seen as describing the only way in which people may work through polarities. Some may begin in different places and switch the middle two stages. Much depends on culture, family upbringing, hormonal levels, sexual orientation, and life experiences. One of the major problems with our current perspectives on gender is our cultural blindness to human difference. The goal for all of us, eventually, is wholeness, but we may start at very different places and go through quite different stages to get there.

Pseudomasculine and Pseudofeminine

Since culture has a very strong impact on all of us through our parental upbringing, teachers and mentors, and the all-pervasive media, many of us are indoctrinated into a rigid, stereotypical version of ourselves based on our sexual equipment. Gender roles may have reflected a reasonable division of labor between men and women in hunting-and-gathering or agricultural societies, and at times they may even help some of us in dealing with one another in everyday interchanges. However, when these roles become rigid, inflexible, and irrelevant to modern life, they become caricatures that have lost their usefulness. These overblown versions of ways to be male or female limit our humanity rather than guide us in our lives, and they have, through the media and other cultural institutions, become grotesque and one-dimensional.

We use the prefix *pseudo–* to emphasize the falseness that gender stereotypes bring to our personalities. These stereotypes are usually a twisting or exaggerating of natural qualities. For instance, power may become "power over" rather than "power for," and reflection may become self-absorption rather than thoughtfulness. From these distortions of natural aspects of gender polarities come stereotypes that cast men as domineering and women as self-centered. Many of our cultural icons, either real or fictitious, are men or women who have lost sight of their true natures and are acting out the group myth of what it is to be a man or woman. The driven, often psychologically wounded lone-wolf warrior/cowboy of television and film is a sad commentary on our view of the masculine, just as the seductive, clinging, or helpless siren depicted in popular culture is a grotesque caricature of the nature of the feminine.

The pseudomasculine and pseudofeminine cultural ideals present false pictures of reality in at least two ways. First, they make it appear that men, in order to be real men, must be totally masculine and not a blend of characteristics; a parallel expectation holds true for women. Those who step out of the mold are often viewed in a negative light. Second, these cultural models hold out a false ideal. Being only half-formed is seen as the ideal, while the possibility of becoming a complex, whole human being is seldom recognized.

People stuck in the pseudo phase are rejecting the opposite polarity within themselves and in others. Much of the impetus for the "war between the sexes" and our overreaction against those who violate the sexual norms comes from our rejection of anything that reminds us of our disowned qualities. As soon as we embrace our own complexity, we become far more accepting of others.

Incorporating the "Other"

People begin the process of spiritual growth from different places. Men, especially men raised by single-parent mothers, may begin this process with a primary identification with the feminine. Women, often those with strong fathers, may identify with the masculine. Yet men and women such as these often become wounded by the pseudomasculine and pseudofeminine culture around them. They may be seen as less worthy or marginal by many in their surroundings. The positive for these individuals is that they have less to unlearn in their process of self-discovery.

Those who are thrust into the pseudomasculine and pseudofeminine roles through their experiences in childhood and adolescence are confronted quite quickly by opportunities to move beyond the stereotypes. First, education places the pseudomasculine male into a confrontation with learning that will not only require him to learn to receive information, but in college and postgraduate work, will also expect him to reflect upon what he has received. Receptivity and reflection are both aspects of the divine feminine. As college professors, we see daily the struggle experienced by young men caught in the clutches of pseudomasculinity. If there is a single reason that underlies the failure of many young men to take full advantage of educational opportunities today, it is the anti-intellectual nature of the pseudomasculine ideal. For the young woman caught in the pseudofeminine trap, education opens the door to the power to determine her own future. The choice is no longer to go from her father's house to her husband's house, but rather to become independent and make her own decision about whether to share her life with another. Education also prepares a young woman to take responsibility within the workplace. Through the process of education, the young woman discovers the masculine qualities of power and responsibility that can free her from pseudofemininity.

Loving relationships are another natural life occurrence that propels men and women toward the other halves of themselves. Feelings of love and tenderness and the desire to put the other first, as well as the vulnerability required by love, are often new and frightening to the pseudomasculine male. These are also the very experiences that save a young man from the arid life of power and mind alone. Emotions are the gift and the crucible of life, but men who embrace only a partial life avoid them as much as possible. Love is often the first call to wholeness, and because of the great power that love has to change us, it may be a young man's best hope for growth. Just as love can pull the man inward and away from his pursuit of meaningless desires and goals, love can pull the pseudofeminine woman out of her inward, reflective self-absorption. She may now become other-oriented, at least for a while. She may enter the male psyche through her loved one and temporarily leave the group of "girls" who have been supporting her pseudofemininity, just as he, like Peter Pan, may leave his group of "lost boys." Even though many loves don't endure, both men and women are better off for having loved, because it is love that has made them become more than they had been. (There are exceptions, of course, such as situations in which abuse occurs.) The major risk is for those who refuse to love again because the pain of loss was too much the first time. These wounded ones may deny themselves the opportunity to learn the next lesson of love.

Life itself is the best teacher of wholeness. If we, male or female, remain open to what our job, family, friends, and activities ask of us, usually we will be propelled toward learning qualities that we haven't yet actualized. The trick is to remain open to what is being asked of us by life. There never arrives a time when we have fulfilled our potential completely, as there is always a next step. Given the scenario that we have been outlining, when you become comfortable with your contrasexual side, you will need to discover the authentic nature of the side of your being that corresponds to your biological gender.

True Masculinity and Femininity

We must remember that we are not implying that men have to be masculine and women must be feminine. We are instead referring to a process of discovery that calls men and women to discover all aspects of themselves. This process leads from a false self through the discovery of two very complex and multifaceted sides of the human being. Men and women may not start this process in parallel places, and it is quite common for some to live most of their lives in the pseudomasculine or pseudofeminine role. Some persons who have had extremely good role models, especially a same-sex parent, may have incorporated a very healthy understanding of how to be an adult of their particular gender.

Those of us who have not had that experience may have to discover these qualities for ourselves.

Given the extent to which pseudomasculinity and pseudofemininity dominate Western culture, finding role models or even allusions to what it means to be authentically masculine or authentically feminine may be a daunting task. However you experience being fully yourself, that is who you are, and it is good. But what we are looking for is a more authentic version of the part of your personality that corresponds to your actual gender. There are very deep truths associated with masculine energy and feminine energy, and the discovery of these components of our full personalities is part of our progress toward wholeness. One method for finding the authentic masculine or feminine within is to find exemplars and role models who will point the way toward finding your own version of your gender. Another way is to peel away the layers of unauthenticity through spiritual practice, until you find the core of your being and start to live from that authentic place. In that case, you will be in touch with what is *real* about both sides of your being.

The Mystery of the Conjunction of Opposites

You may think that what we have been exploring in this chapter is not very spiritual because it is mostly about psychological and social role change, but the opposite is actually true. The integration of your inner masculine and feminine natures is the great work of a lifetime and is at the heart of creating a personality capable of spiritual realization. It is similar to putting two active chemicals together; when they mix, they create a third substance. So it is with the "alchemical marriage" of masculine and feminine energies within you. The result of this marriage is that you will become a human being who is very unlike most other human beings. It is not an exaggeration to state that at the core of all spiritual paths is the same purpose: the wholeness that comes from the reconciliation of the opposites within.

Exercise: Alchemical Marriage

It is easier and more productive to embrace your full potential through love than to accept it through guilt. For this reason, finding your disowned qualities through seeing them in an idealized other may be not only healing but also joyful. Use the mirrors that we describe below to discover the contrasexual side of yourself, the part of your being that you have been seeking for lifetimes.

- Do you have an idealized image of the perfect mate? Most people do, but they are usually unaware of it and project this image onto people they fall in love with. Attempt to make this image conscious by purposefully imagining who the perfect mate would be, even if you already have a mate. (This is a symbolic practice, so it should not harm your existing relationship.)

- If the above practice is difficult for you, think about the people you fall in love with. What qualities seem most pronounced? What qualities do those whom you have been in love with share? Don't limit yourself to thinking about the obvious or only the good qualities, but instead look at the whole picture. For instance, are you a woman who gets romantically involved with men who want to dominate or limit you? Maybe you are trying to find your own power and control. Are you a man who finds women who mother you? Maybe you are trying to connect with your own nurturing nature or your vulnerability.

- After you have explored your ideal and the qualities you seek, imagine a person who embodies the perfection of those qualities. Make the image as real and as alive as you can. Now imagine that you are with this person in the presence of a great spiritual being, who marries the two of you.

- Now imagine making such exquisite love to this person that your bodies, minds, hearts, and souls merge into a single, complete, and authentic being.

- Keeping this image alive in your heart will assist you in growing into what you have imagined.

We have explored a few of the avenues that you may take to work toward becoming a whole person. A person experiences this wholeness of being, the "alchemical marriage," as an integration of the left and right sides of the body, the ability to balance the solar and lunar aspects of one's being, the capacity to act as well as the capacity to reflect, and the wish both to give and to receive. While these outcomes may sound somewhat prosaic, in actuality this stage of development may bring with it a burst of energy, a sense of radiant well-being, and an inner peacefulness. You may feel alive as never before, despite the challenges of everyday life, and people will probably tell you that you somehow seem more *real* than many others.

sixteen

The Transformative Power of Relationships

The path of love may be the most powerful path for many of us. We live immersed in networks of relationships. They provide nourishment for our lives, and we in turn nourish others with our caring. Sometimes, it is true, our relationships may be sources of pain as well as love, and at times we may want nothing more than to escape them. We struggle with our friends, relatives, lovers, spouses, or partners on a daily basis. If you are in the midst of such a struggle, you may wonder how relationships possibly could help you in your spiritual development. If you are happily involved in a loving relationship, then the notion of relationships as a tool for transformation may make more sense. Surprisingly, our experience tells us that the painful struggles, as well as the loving moments, can be used for growth—if we are aware of what we are doing. *Awareness* is the key here, and it is not easy!

Deep, committed relationships may be a wonderful vehicle for doing this work, and they provide a safe and trusting milieu for both enlarging the heart and clearing out baggage. When we found each other, the love we shared was overwhelmingly strong, and so were the challenges. A relationship like ours that has deep spiritual roots often seems to carry lifetimes of baggage to be worked out. Our early relationship was like a roller coaster, moving from loving bliss to painful conflict. Because both of us were committed to the relationship, we stuck it out, even though each of us at times wondered privately what we had gotten ourselves into. Our marriage was a crucible for the purification of our hearts and the realization of love, and now, despite the hard times, both of us are grateful that we followed the path of love. You might be glad to know that once we developed more mastery over our powerful emotions, the struggles subsided, and the loving, supportive times became the norm, as is common in this sort of relationship.

At a certain point, you will realize that what we call love in the English language is actually much more than what we generally understand as love. Love is the glue that holds the universe together. It contains the light and life force that hold the atoms together, it holds the natural world together, and it holds loving humans together. Sufis use the term *ishk* to convey this concept, and they say that *ishk* is "Love, Lover, and Beloved"—*all* of it! The realization of this beautiful thought leads straight to an understanding of the nature of the universe. When we clear out our hearts, awaken them with love, and allow them to become larger and larger, we are then transformed. Ultimately, there are no more dualities, only the unity of Love, Lover, and Beloved, all made of the same stuff—and we are one with it.

Practicing Radical Presence

How do we develop the capacity to be with another person in a way that allows us to experience a taste of *ishk*, that deep universal love that unites all of us? One way to begin is to practice being absolutely present in the moment with just one other person. The term that has come to us for this experience is *radical presence*, which implies that this is something different from and much deeper than our usual ways of relating to others in everyday life. *Ishk* is not gushy, and neither is radical presence. When we let go of the incessant stream of thought that occupies our minds, we are more able to attend to the other in a quiet, grounded way. *Listening* and *being* are the core skills leading to the capacity for radical presence.

Often, we think we are listening to others, but we may hear only partially what they are trying to convey to us, because we are preoccupied. What grabs our minds away from our intention to be with others? Most of us have a thousand worries, a thousand things we think we should have done yesterday. Beyond these, often we are thinking about how we are going to respond to the other. How will we answer the implied question? How will we show that we know what the person is talking about? How will we gain the upper hand in the common game of one-upmanship? The exercise at the end of this chapter will help you learn the basics of radical presence, a first step toward building a beautiful connection with another person, whether it lasts for a few minutes or a lifetime.

Being with another person involves the ability to let go of your agenda, ideas, and perspectives and just be there in the moment. To allow yourself to be unguarded and authentic when you are with someone you care about creates the radical presence that we are talking about. You may suddenly realize a truth about the depths of that person's reality that may stun you with its beauty or its pain as you open your hearts to each other. Whether the experience reveals beauty or pain—or an entirely different quality— keeping your awareness in the heart center brings harmony and peace to the encounter.

This leads us to an important point to remember when practicing radical presence: this only works when our motives are clear and pure. You cannot make this sort of deep connection when you want something from the other, as wanting distorts the relationship. The only goal that works is simply to be present with another human being, to understand that person in a deep way, and to share the moment together.

We have had amazing experiences related to this kind of presence, as you may already have had as well. Some of the most powerful experiences have been cross-cultural encounters, as these require us to transcend additional boundaries. Jan returns to a moment that provides an example of such an encounter and experience:

> Once, when backpacking in the foothills of the Himalayas, I paused to rest, leaning against a rock wall by the trail. A tiny, ancient-appearing woman dressed in a worn but colorful sari came by and stopped in front of me, looking up and smiling broadly. "Ahcha!" she said. Delighted, but not knowing how to respond, I gazed into her deep, kind eyes and repeated, "Ahcha!" back to her. We stood there together, smiling and exchanging "ahchas" for what seemed like a long time—or maybe no time at all. Then, as quickly as she came, she grinned and gave me the traditional greeting, bowing with hands together. I returned the gesture, and she left. I glowed with the joy of this encounter for the rest of the day, and I still find my heart warming as I write about it. Since that time, friends from India have told me that "ahcha" is an all-purpose word that conveys the meaning "All right!" or "OK!" or a number of similar positive thoughts.

You never know when such an encounter will happen, nor can you predict who the other will be. One night, at the wedding reception of one of our graduates, we were delighted to run into a former student, who was holding her little twenty-six-month-old son, whom we'd never met before. The little guy reached out and grabbed Jan, with his arms tight around her neck, and hung on in one of the sweetest embraces that Jan had ever experienced. His mother was flabbergasted, saying that he was usually quite reticent with strangers, but here he was, just hanging on as if he and Jan were long-lost friends. The embrace lasted several minutes, and then it was over and he went back to his mom.

Other moments of radical presence may mark the beginning of a great friendship, a fine working relationship, or perhaps a deep love affair. Whatever the outcome, the beauty of it is that two human beings have managed to be with each other in a way that transcends differences and affirms their common humanity.

Pregnancy and Parenthood

Getting pregnant may not be seen as a particularly spiritual undertaking in Western societies, nor is being pregnant viewed as a wonderful state by every woman. From our perspective, both are marvelous opportunities to bring spirituality into your life at a deep level. Conceiving a baby can come about accidentally as a result of a glorious—or not so glorious—sexual encounter, can happen as a rationally planned event, or can be done with full consciousness of the spiritual significance of creating a new life. If you would like to follow the latter path, you and your partner may wish to spend time together thinking about the meaning of bringing this child into the world. If both of you have learned how to meditate, that is a great vehicle for getting clear about intention and timing. When you feel that the time is right, you might decide to meditate or to listen to uplifting music before making love. You might think of yourselves as being conduits for this new being to enter into life on this planet, and you might also visualize yourselves as the creators of a beautiful accommodation, a welcoming abode for this new spirit. You may invite a being to come into your lives and make a conscious vow to nurture and protect it. We have known several people who were able to intuit the presence of their child-to-be hanging around them even before the conception. Conceiving in this way can be a tremendous gift to all involved, but if it happens in a less conscious way, don't be concerned. Often, your deep inner intention will have the same effect as a more conscious effort. You still may approach the pregnancy with as much awareness and love as possible, and your baby will feel that on a deep level.

For women, pregnancy is also an opportunity for conscious work with yourself as well as with the developing little one. If you see your body and spirit as a home for the new child, you will do everything you can to keep it healthy and to keep yourself in a state that is as calm and happy as possible. Modern science is beginning to confirm that babies in the womb respond to their mothers' states, so keeping your consciousness as high and clear as possible is a good goal. It is true that pregnancy can be a challenging time physically and emotionally for some women—every woman is different—but for many, it can be a lovely time of feeling like a co-creator of life. I remember feeling amazingly in tune with the universe during my pregnancies, and even labor and delivery, though challenging at times, were part of a miracle.

There are spiritual practices that you can do during your pregnancy to enhance the experience. Visualizing light pouring down upon you and the baby is wonderful. You may also visualize all the abundance of the creation nurturing you and the baby. A good way to do the latter is to visualize a beautiful river of sparkling clear water coming down from a mountain and flowing in front of you from left to right (the direction of bringing things into manifestation). Feel the energy of the river bringing everything that you and the baby need to grow and thrive.

Another lovely practice is to think of a nurturing, caring woman, whether someone in your own life or someone you have read about. It could be your grandmother or a favorite aunt, or it could be a more well-known spiritual being, such as Mother Theresa, the Virgin of Guadalupe, the White Buffalo Woman, or Kuan Yin, the Buddhist incarnation of compassion. Visualize that being holding you in her arms, loving you, stroking your forehead, or singing gently to you. Ask her for whatever you need, and have confidence that she will in some way respond to you lovingly. Jan remembers a time when her life was feeling a bit rough:

> I sat down to meditate and was amazed that before my inner eyes there appeared a tremendous gathering of women. One strong, gentle, and compassionate woman stood at the front of the gathering, and then behind her, in a gigantic triangular shape extending farther than I could see, were women from many cultures and many eras. Some of them I rec-

ognized from stories and photos, and some were totally unknown to me, but all of them were there to comfort and encourage me. The memory of that experience is still alive for me, and I know, many years later, that these women are still available for encouragement, wisdom, and inspiration. I know beyond a doubt that the universe contains so many beings on inner planes who are just waiting to be of service to us when the going gets rough—or when we need a little comfort and guidance.

For fathers, pregnancy may be a time of excitement and exhilaration as well as a time of confusion and ambiguity. It may be hard to know what your role is, and it is common to feel somewhat left out of the picture. It is important for women to include the fathers in the planning and also in the spiritual attunement to the growth of the baby, and it is important for fathers to volunteer to participate in this work. Sitting together to meditate or to listen to music is a great practice. If you sit quietly, facing each other, you may visualize that you two are gradually creating a strong, bright, protective aura around the baby. That bright aura will stay with the little one as he grows and will serve him well even after birth. You can also enhance the baby's aura by facing one another while you sleep at night, at least part of the time.

The first few weeks of a baby's life are often a crucial time for the father, since this is a time when the man's role in the family may either diminish or grow, depending on his ability to open his heart. He will grow by learning the humility necessary to put aside his own needs and widen his heart to his wife and child, and he should recognize that while the bond between the two of them is incredibly powerful, his bond with both of them is vital and is built, strengthened, and maintained through love.

As your children grow, the relationship between you and them can become another vehicle for spiritual development. Relationships may be both strong and delicate, and the parent-child relationship is one that provides a lifeline for the child and an opportunity for transformation for parents. New mothers—and fathers as well—often are amazed by the degree to which they forget themselves as they put the baby's needs ahead of any of their own desires. Having or adopting a baby is a natural way to learn to let go of one's own less-important wishes and to put another human first. New parents easily release unnecessary, ego-serving desires as they focus on keeping their babies healthy and contented.

We easily could write another book on parenting as part of the path of relationships. For now, let's explore a few examples of how this might work. Spending time playing with your children, reading to them, singing to them and with them, and talking with them about what matters to them—all of these are ways in which one can practice radical presence. Jan learned when her children were toddlers that when they started to whine, usually her attention had drifted from the heart connection between them. All it took to remedy the situation was to refocus on that heart connection, something one can feel, and attend to their needs.

It didn't have to take a long time, but they needed to know that the connection was still strong. She also reminded them gently that they did not have to use the whining voice, that she preferred a direct statement of their needs. They seldom whined, and mother and children retained their close connections.

One may learn how to use parenting experiences to deepen spiritual growth in other ways as well, as the following story from Jan shows:

> When they were small, my sons loved to be sung to sleep, after the bedtime stories, of course. Often, by the time we got to the singing stage, I was exhausted, and as much as I loved my sons, I was ready to fall into bed myself—without a song and without meditating. Then it hit me that I could sing to them some of the lovely meditative chants I had learned—and it would benefit all of us. This became one of my favorite spiritual practices for several years.

Another experience of Jan's that combined practical parenting with real spiritual growth occurred many years ago at the first three-week-long meditation workshop she ever attended:

> I was struggling to cope with the realities of camping in the woods in the rain with my two small, enthusiastic sons, who at the time were two and four years old. I had to miss many of the sessions, because the incessant rain forced the closing of the children's camp, which they were to attend for part of each day.

My younger son was determined to walk, rather than be carried, on the steep, rocky, muddy trails, and he kept tripping over the rocks and landing in the mud. After fifteen minutes on the trail, he was usually mud from head to toe, and I was running out of clean clothes for him. That was just the beginning of the frustrations. The most difficult part was missing the lectures on meditation that my heart yearned for intensely. One day, an older woman, who obviously had been meditating for many years, stopped and asked how things were going. She advised, "Just go back to your tent and look into your children's eyes, and you'll get higher than you ever would meditating." I followed her advice and have been grateful to her ever since that day. She pointed the way for making parenthood a spiritual practice, and it has been a tremendous gift.

Starting from birth, parents can practice looking at their children with the eyes of the heart, rather than solely with the outer eyes. Observe your child's inner being, and look for the hidden qualities within that child that are just waiting to manifest themselves. You might see that one child has deep wisdom hidden in her heart, or perhaps you will notice that another child has the gift of creativity. You may be delighted to realize that your child has a wonderful capacity to see the humor in life and that his joy is a gift to all around him. Many children carry the seeds of gentle caring, and they are tuned in to all sorts of creatures, from bugs to pets to birds. Perhaps your child is more serious and has a deep desire to learn and understand. Of course, all children carry a multitude of qualities within, and as parents you have the opportunity to use your creativity to help them find ways to express these gifts.

One of the most important ways to nurture your children's qualities is to give them the gift of time to hang out and explore their environments. We tend to overprogram our children's lives, and some children have little time to use their imaginations in creative play, which is the work of children. You may give them access to simple toys that they can use in their own ways—expensive, sophisticated toys are not necessary.

As your children grow, you may be aware of their developmental needs, and that includes their spiritual needs. Addressing children's spiritual growth is an immense topic. We will content ourselves with pointing out that children often are attuned to deep spiritual realities, and they may teach us, just as we teach them. Being with our children in Nature, for example, gives us an opportunity to reconnect with realities that we may have forgotten.

EXERCISE: PRACTICING RADICAL PRESENCE

To do this exercise, you will need to find a friend or partner who is willing to spend a little time with you.

- Find a comfortable place where you will not be interrupted, and sit together on the floor or ground or on straight-backed chairs. Turn off the phone, the television, and anything else that might disturb you.

- Sit facing each other as close as you feel comfortable.

- Gaze softly into each other's eyes (not staring) for a few moments. If you begin to feel uncomfortable, shift your gaze to the center of the other's forehead, just above the eyes, and unfocus your eyes a bit. If you feel the impulse to giggle or laugh, let it go and return to the gaze. You may close your eyes briefly if that helps you to stay centered and to maintain the contact.

- Allow your conscious mind and your heart to attune to the atmosphere of your friend or partner, and be receptive to noticing the positive qualities that are coming through this person.

- Let your conscious mind and your heart gently focus on feeling a quality that lies deep within the other, perhaps a positive quality that this person has not yet fully manifested. Stay with this for a few minutes, remembering that this is a receptive process, not an active one.

- When both are ready, take turns sharing what you experienced. Briefly describe to each other the qualities that you felt in the other, and listen to the person's response to that feedback. Perhaps this is something that your friend or partner has felt as well, or it may be new. If either of you is uncomfortable with the content of your sharing, let it go. Perhaps the information will help the other in beginning to express the latent quality.

- Thank each other, and share a hug, if you like!

After completing this exercise with your friend or partner, you may expect to feel closer to that person and more capable of being totally present in the moment with others. You may think of several variations on this theme. After some practice, you may find that you naturally tune in to people whom you meet on a deeper level. You will be able to sense who they are, the condition of their hearts, and what they need.

There is one condition to this work. This depth of knowing calls for profound respect for the dignity of all people, as well as the capacity to guard others' secrets scrupulously. A personal commitment to keeping what you know about others *completely confidential* is paramount as you open your heart and mind to people on deeper levels. Totally avoiding gossip will protect others, and it will build your own magnetism.

Through the practice of radical presence, you will begin to deepen your participation in *ishk*, universal love, as "Love, Lover, and Beloved." There may be moments of truth when you will understand what it means to become the eyes and the heart of the One Life, whose energies are flowing through you with every breath you take.

seventeen

Living from the Heart

Now that you have read about many different aspects of spiritual development, you may ask, "How does all of this come together in my life?" or "How do I make it real?" Figuring out where to start may be a challenge, but we suggest, "Start anywhere!" Take one step, and you will find that doors will begin to open for you. Try out the exercises from any of the chapters in the book, or use your own intuition about the place where you would like to start. One beautiful thing about spiritual development is that it is a holistic endeavor, so by starting with virtually any aspect of spirituality, you will be led to further steps. Synchronicity will speed up for you, and you will meet people and find resources that you didn't know existed. Almost everyone we know who has been on a spiritual journey for a time has marvelous stories about their journey's unfolding. If one door closes, another door opens. Your intention to grow will carry you forward, and the universe will open its arms to meet you more than halfway.

You may predict that your life will change, often in unexpected ways. You will find that some things that used to matter to you will lose their importance, and other things will become more important. Some activities, desires, or preoccupations may fall away, and others may take their places. After a while, you may find that some friends do not seem as close as they used to, and you may meet others who share more interests with you. As we mentioned early in this book, your perspectives, as well as your priorities, will change. The nature of life on this planet is constant change, and the more you are able to let go of your unnecessary attachments, the more easily your life will flow. You might ask, "So how will I get through all of this change?" One of the answers is to stay in the moment, to hone your awareness of the present and to practice just *being here* right now, just as you are, just as the world is. This moment is all that exists, and when you become grounded in this moment, you will be able to move through the changes. The truth is, of course, that your life will change whether or not you decide to take a step in the direction of spiritual development. When you are consciously working *with* the changes, rather than fighting them, you will be able to use life as a teacher and flow with whatever happens.

Living Your Realizations

How you live your life is ultimately the gauge of your spiritual development. The purpose of spiritual work, from one perspective, is to infuse life with spirit and to realize the Oneness of all being. It is not necessary to eschew the world in favor of spiritual realms. This world is the place where our spiritual work must be done. It is here and now that life may become a heaven on earth. The way in which you may accomplish this great work is through the awakening of your heart and mind—the essence of spiritual development.

You might wonder, "How can I live a truly spiritual life in a world that is so full of ugliness, pain, and despair?" How do any of us live authentic, deep lives in societies that value unauthenticity and shallowness? If it were easy, it would not involve so much unlearning of old ways. If it were easy, all of us would be doing it, and the world would be a transformed place. While spiritual development is deeply satisfying, it takes years of unfolding to live a deeply authentic spiritual life. In reality, you need not look so far down the road. Spiritual development is about beginning to live each moment from the heart rather than waiting to be fully awake or enlightened at some future time. This is done by developing spiritual qualities in your everyday life. The purpose of our discussions of qualities such as wisdom, joy, mastery, insight, compassion, and love is to encourage you to begin to develop and to live these qualities in your life in the world. We might view these qualities as vehicles for manifesting aspects of the One Being in our lives, a way of bringing spirit into life. There is no need to wait until you are an illumined being before you start manifesting these qualities; you may begin right now.

You might find it easier to incorporate spiritual practices into your life and to develop more spiritual qualities if you were able to change your self-image. The will may be used consciously to direct this effort. *You have the power to begin to see yourself as a spiritual person, a being of light, right now!* If you decide that developing as a spiritual being is your deepest desire, you will increasingly view yourself in that way. It may be at times difficult, because so many things and so many people will want to pull you in other directions, but it also will be a deeply satisfying choice. In esoteric schools, people often get new names that will remind them of who they are becoming, but you instead may hold silently in your heart the intention to be a spiritual being.

EXERCISE: THE PLEDGE

A tradition in the Zoroastrian religion is to remember, as the first thing when awakening in the morning, that you play a part in the cosmic struggle between good and evil. The primary goal is to work for Light over darkness, Truth over falsehood, and order over chaos. People accomplish this pledge by repeating the Persian equivalent of "I Will" several times upon rising.

You may now do something similar—but without the emphasis on cosmic struggle. You may remind yourself every morning when you get up of your desire to be a truly spiritual person.

- Begin by remembering your intention to place your spiritual development at the forefront of your life.

- Now repeat, "I Will!" seven times, each time remembering your commitment to Light, Truth, and Love.

This practice can be very powerful and life-changing, so guard it closely. Some practices such as this are very delicate and need to be kept secret, because if you tell another person who might laugh or ridicule the practice, it may lose its power to impact your changing personality.

The Next Steps of Your Journey

In *Authentic Spirituality*, Richard discussed creating personality as one of the primary tasks of spiritual development. The book described qualities related to wisdom, such as discernment, perspective, and understanding, as well as qualities related to love, such as kindness, compassion, and magnanimity. Many other important and transformative qualities exist.

If you wish to continue your journey of spiritual development, one of the next steps is to nurture and develop the qualities that you need to manifest in your life, starting with just one. You will be on your way to becoming that which you seek. Self-realization always has been seen as the primary goal on spiritual paths, but the self that is realized is the perfected self, the self that has become a mirror of the Divine. You may ask, "How can I accomplish this enormous task when I don't even know what that latent part of me is like?" You may wonder if, given the limitations of the mind, you might misunderstand the true nature of wisdom and love. We have a suggestion that will assist you in overcoming these limitations: begin to bring more balance and refinement into your life.

Balance

During our seven-week stay in Bali, Indonesia, we were struck by the ever-present black-and-white checkered cloths and flags that were found particularly around temples, worn by dancers in the barong dance, and even wrapped around statues. We discovered that these flags represent the balancing of all the forces of life, positive and negative, good and evil. Balinese people believe that much of their spiritual work on earth is to maintain the delicate balance of life's polarities, and they take this seriously. The women of the villages spend hours virtually every morning creating beautiful offerings of fruit, rice cakes, and symbolic substances to carry to the temples, and they also make small offerings to throw out to the trouble-making forces to keep them from making mischief. We found that living in such a harmonious culture had a profound effect on us, and we began to understand the importance of balance in an entirely new way. You may find it helpful to remember the importance of balance in your life as well, when you are trying to figure out what path to take, which people to believe, and what choices to make. You will be saved from going too far astray if you remember to balance your knowledge with love, power with wisdom, and action with reflection.

You also may wonder how much energy you need to put into work and other so-called worldly pursuits and how much energy you need to put into your spiritual development. The immediate answer is, again, to pay attention to balancing the two, although the answer may evolve until your worlds come together. At that point, you may find that your work has become a vehicle for manifesting your love. If you are able to keep a balance between the various demands in your life, it is likely that your entire life will become a spiritual practice—that everything you do will be related to your spiritual development. But balance is a tough goal to achieve. As soon as the frenetic pace of the modern workplace begins to gobble up too much of your life's energy, you may lose your balance and the worlds will become separate again. Look at every aspect of your life and check whether there is balance among your various pursuits; if so, then you are heading in the right direction. If balance is lacking, then it is time to use spiritual practices to gain perspective and insight regarding possible ways to make some changes. Life is a great teacher!

Before we leave this discussion of balance, we need to point out that there are exceptions to our thoughts about balance. Sometimes life will pull you out of your safe zone and push you into what might feel like a very unbalanced place for a while. This is sometimes the way that major changes announce themselves. Each of us has found ourself taking on major professional responsibilities that seemed to be shifting the balance in our lives from the spiritual to the material. However, as these changes played themselves out, we discovered that life was stretching us so that we could become stronger and wiser people and that the balance eventually returned—but at a new level. Remember that your mind is not always aware of what is going on; sometimes what is needed is trust. The emphasis that many religions have placed on faith carries a deep wisdom that relates to this sort of dilemma.

Refinement

A second important consideration when monitoring your spiritual development is refinement. Coarseness, dullness, and heaviness in mind and manner drag us down, and refinement, clarity, and lightness of spirit speed our journeys. Refinement is at the heart of many of the changes you may make in your consciousness, as well as in your emotions and even your physical being. In a world where the ideals held out to you by many of our leaders and by the media often involve gross, angry, and very unrefined ways of being, it may be difficult to become more sensitive and refined, yet this is the task of a spiritual person. Without refinement and the various qualities associated with it, such as sensitivity, clarity, subtlety, and lightness, your spiritual development will stall. If you find that your job, certain activities, or specific people cause you to appear more gross, this is a strong indication that changes are needed. There are times when your spiritual path must take precedence over situations that do not allow you to progress. When you need to evaluate how your journey is unfolding, look closely at whether or not your consciousness is becoming more refined. If you have some trusted people in your life, perhaps a spiritual guide, ask those people as well, because it is the nature of our own preoccupied minds to tell us what we want to hear and not necessarily what is true.

Living with Paradox and Uncertainty

Another discovery you may make is that life on this planet is ultimately full of paradoxes. We cannot capture Truth in a box, as the nature of reality is much more complex than that. Being able to live with uncertainty, to live with the knowledge that what you understand as Truth will, at each step of the way, unfold into a deeper, higher, broader understanding of reality, is a challenge. At each point, you will probably look back and exclaim, "I wish I had known this before!" Then things will change again, unless you are content to remain at a certain level. You may expect some tough times, you may expect to make mistakes, but you may also expect increased joy, peace, love, harmony, and beauty in your life.

Are the rewards of this path worth the inner work it involves? If we could go back in time, would we start the journey again? Our answer is a resounding, "Yes, the beauty of this journey is certainly worth the work it involves, and you bet we would do it all over again!" In reality, the path of spiritual development is more about unfolding and relaxing, enfolded in the compassionate arms of the universe, than it is about work. It is about the freedom of your soul, about releasing your soul from the confines of concepts and perceived limitations. There comes a point at which the spiritual journey is the most important aspect of life, because it encompasses all of your life. There is nothing that is not related, because all of life is One Life. We are swimming in a vast ocean of Oneness, and we share the same precious water. All of us are connected, every molecule is connected, and in the final analysis, we share a common fate. When you arrive at that realization, you may find it a bit hard to focus on the everyday tasks of life, but life goes on, and each of us still has to pull our own weight. Some of the advanced stages of the journey call for you to live in the world as ordinary people, carrying with you the stunning knowledge of the Unity of all existence. You may be tempted to see others who appear to be at earlier stages of the journey as not being evolved, or you may see them as puppets of life, unaware of the nature of existence.

How might you avoid the twin dangers of aloofness and arrogance at this stage? The answer lies in the opening of the heart. When your heart is cleaned out, alive, and open, compassion floods your being, and there is no way that you will be able to judge others. You will see others far more clearly and deeply than you ever expected, but your seeing will be tempered by deep love and the knowledge that all of us are pieces of the One Being in disguise. Each of us performs a vital part in the great play of life, and we will have to wait to know exactly how the next act will unfold. There is tremendous joy in taking the leap of faith to make the next step. May your journey be joyous and fruitful, and may you realize your deepest heart's desire, the purpose of your life.

Works Cited

Harner, Michael. 1990. *The Way of the Shaman.* San Francisco: Harper & Row.

Johnston, William, ed. 1973. *The Cloud of Unknowing and the Book of Privy Counseling.* New York: Image/Doubleday.

Pinkola Estés, Clarissa. 1992. *Women Who Run with the Wolves.* New York: Ballantine.

Reps, Paul. 1989. *Zen Flesh, Zen Bones.* Garden City, NY: Anchor.

Selected Bibliography

The following books may be helpful in pursuing further information about topics that we have discussed in *Spiritual Development for Beginners*.

General Spirituality

Dass, Ram. *Be Here Now.* New York: Crown Publishing, 1971.

Grof, Christina, and Stanislav Grof. *The Stormy Search for the Self: A Guide to Personal Growth through Transformational Crisis.* Los Angeles: Jeremy P. Tarcher, Inc., 1990.

Kornfield, Jack. *After the Ecstasy, the Laundry: How the Heart Grows Wise on the Spiritual Path.* New York: Bantam, 2000.

Potter, Richard. *Authentic Spirituality: The Direct Path to Consciousness.* St. Paul, MN: Llewellyn Publications, 2004.

Tolle, Eckhart. *The Power of Now: A Guide to Spiritual Enlightenment.* Novato, CA: New World Library, 1999.

Wilber, Ken. *The Essential Ken Wilber: An Introductory Reader.* Boston: Shambhala, 1998.

Western Perspectives

Belenky, Mary, Blythe Clinchy, Nancy Goldberg, and Jill Tarule. *Women's Ways of Knowing: The Development of Self, Voice, and Mind.* New York: Basic Books, 1997.

Bly, Robert. *A Little Book on the Human Shadow.* San Francisco: Harper & Row, 1988.

Campbell, Joseph. *Thou Art That: Transforming Religious Metaphor.* Novato, CA: New World Library, 2001.

———. *Transformations of Myth through Time.* New York: Harper & Row, 1990.

Christ, Carol P., and Judith Plaskow, eds. *Womanspirit Rising: A Feminist Reader in Religion.* San Francisco, HarperSanFrancisco, 1979.

Edinger, Edward F. *The Creation of Consciousness: Jung's Myth for Modern Man.* Toronto: Inner City Books, 1984.

Fowler, James W. *Stages of Faith: The Psychology of Human Development and the Quest for Meaning.* San Francisco: HarperSanFrancisco, 1995.

Gray, William G. *Western Inner Workings.* York Beach, ME: Samuel Weiser, 1983.

Griffin, Emilie, ed. *The Cloud of Unknowing.* San Francisco: HarperSanFrancisco, 1981.

Hauck, Dennis William. *The Emerald Tablet: Alchemy for Personal Transformation.* New York: Penguin/Arkana, 1999.

Kadloubovsky, E., and G. E. H. Palmer, trans. *Writings from the Philokalia on the Prayer of the Heart.* London: Faber and Faber, 1979.

Knight, Gareth. *A Practical Guide to Qabalistic Symbolism.* York Beach, ME: Samuel Weiser, 1965.

Matthews, Caitlin, and John Matthews. *The Western Way: A Practical Guide to the Western Mystery Tradition.* 2 vols. London: Arkana, 1985.

Meade, Michael. *Men and the Water of Life.* San Francisco: HarperSanFrancisco, 1993.

Merton, Thomas. *Contemplative Prayer.* New York: Doubleday, 1996.

Nouwen, Henri. *Spiritual Direction: Wisdom for the Long Walk of Faith.* New York: HarperCollins, 2006.

———. *The Wounded Healer.* New York: Doubleday, 1979.

Pinkola Estés, Clarissa. *Women Who Run with the Wolves.* New York: Ballantine, 1992.

Progoff, Ira, trans. *The Cloud of Unknowing.* New York: Dell Publishing, 1957.

Teresa of Avila. *The Interior Castle.* Translated by Kieran Kavanaugh and Otilio Rodriguez. New York: Paulist Press, 1979.

Wiesel, Eli. *Souls on Fire.* New York: Simon and Schuster, 1982.

Eastern Perspectives

Byrom, Thomas. *The Heart of Awareness: A Translation of the Ashtavakra Gita.* Boston: Shambhala, 1990.

Chodron, Pema. *The Pema Chodron Collection.* New York: One Spirit, 2003.

Evans-Wentz, W. Y. *The Tibetan Book of the Great Liberation.* Oxford: Oxford University Press, 1968.

Hanh, Thich Nhat. *The Heart of the Buddha's Teaching: Transforming Suffering into Peace, Joy, and Liberation.* New York: Broadway Books, 1998.

————. *Living Buddha, Living Christ.* New York: Riverhead Books, 1995.

Kornfield, Jack. *A Path with Heart: A Guide through the Perils and Promises of Spiritual Life.* New York: Bantam Books, 1993.

Muktananda, Swami. *Play of Consciousness.* San Francisco: Harper & Row, 1978.

Rinpoche, Sogyal. *The Tibetan Book of Living and Dying.* San Francisco: HarperSanFrancisco, 1992.

Suzuki, Shunryu. *Zen Mind, Beginner's Mind: Informal Talks on Zen Meditation and Practice.* 14th ed. New York: Weatherhill, 1980.

Thurman, Robert. *Infinite Life.* New York: Riverhead Books, 2004.

Trungpa, Chogyam. *Cutting Through Spiritual Materialism.* Berkeley, CA: Shambhala, 1973.

Shamanism

Andrews, Ted. *Animal-Speak: The Spiritual and Magical Powers of Creatures Great and Small.* St. Paul, MN: Llewellyn Publications, 1993.

Cowan, Tom. *Fire in the Head: Shamanism and the Celtic Spirit.* San Francisco: HarperSanFrancisco, 1993.

DeMallie, Raymond J. *The Sixth Grandfather: Black Elk's Teachings Given to John G. Neihardt.* Lincoln, NE: University of Nebraska Press, 1984.

Harner, Michael. *The Way of the Shaman.* San Francisco: Harper & Row, 1990.

Ingerman, Sandra. *Medicine for the Earth: How to Transform Personal and Environmental Toxins.* New York: Three Rivers Press, 2000.

———. *Soul Retrieval: Mending the Fragmented Self.* San Francisco: HarperSanFrancisco, 1991.

Matthews, John. *The Celtic Shaman: A Handbook.* Shaftesbury, UK: Element, 1991.

Neihardt, John G. *Black Elk Speaks.* Lincoln, NE: University of Nebraska Press, 1979.

Prechtel, Martin. *Secrets of the Talking Jaguar: Memoirs from the Living Heart of a Mayan Village.* New York: Jeremy P. Tarcher/Putnam, 1999.

Tedlock, Barbara. *The Woman in the Shaman's Body: Reclaiming the Feminine in Religion and Medicine.* New York: Bantam Books, 2005.

Villoldo, Alberto. *Shaman, Healer, Sage: How to Heal Yourself and Others with the Energy Medicine of the Americas.* New York: Harmony Books, 2000.

Western Sufism

Douglas-Klotz, Neil. *The Sufi Book of Life: 99 Pathways of the Heart for the Modern Dervish.* New York: Penguin Books, 2005.

Inayat Khan, Hazrat. *The Heart of Sufism: Essential Writings of Hazrat Inayat Khan.* Boston: Shambhala, 1999.

———. *The Music of Life.* Santa Fe, NM: Omega Press, 1983.

Inayat Khan, Pir Vilayat. *Awakening: A Sufi Experience.* New York: Jeremy P. Tarcher/Putnam, 1999.

———. *The Message in Our Time.* San Francisco: Harper & Row, 1978.

———. *That Which Transpires Behind That Which Appears: The Experience of Sufism.* New Lebanon, NY: Omega Publications, 1994.

Shah, Idries. *The Way of the Sufi.* New York: E. P. Dutton, 1970.

Poetry

Barks, Coleman. *Delicious Laughter: Rambunctious Teaching Stories from the Mathnawi.* Athens, GA: Maypop Books, 1990.

———, trans. *Feeling the Shoulder of the Lion: Poetry and Teaching Stories of Rumi.* Putney, VT: Threshold Books, 1991.

———. *Rumi: We Are Three.* Athens, GA: Maypop Books, 1987.

Bly, Robert. *The Kabir Book: Forty-Four of the Ecstatic Poems of Kabir.* Boston: Beacon Press, 1977.

———. *The Night Abraham Called to the Stars.* New York: HarperCollins, 2001.

Gibran, Kahlil. *The Prophet.* New York: Alfred A. Knopf, 1981.

Ladinsky, Daniel, trans. *The Gift: Poems by Hafiz, the Great Sufi Master.* New York: Penguin Group, 1999.

———. *I Heard God Laughing: Renderings of Hafiz.* Walnut Creek, CA: Sufism Reoriented, 1996.

Moyne, John, and Coleman Barks. *Open Secret: Versions of Rumi.* Putney, VT: Threshold Books, 1984.

Index

To Write to the Authors

If you wish to contact the authors or would like more information about this book, please write to the authors in care of Llewellyn Worldwide and we will forward your request. Both the authors and publisher appreciate hearing from you and learning of your enjoyment of this book and how it has helped you. Llewellyn Worldwide cannot guarantee that every letter written to the authors can be answered, but all will be forwarded. Please write to:

Richard and Jan Potter
℅ Llewellyn Worldwide
2143 Wooddale Drive, Dept. 0-7387-0750-3
Woodbury, MN 55125-2989, U.S.A.

Please enclose a self-addressed stamped envelope for reply,
or $1.00 to cover costs. If outside U.S.A., enclose
international postal reply coupon.

Many of Llewellyn's authors have websites with additional information and resources. For more information, please visit our website at:

www.llewellyn.com